P

A Place of Refuge

That is the simple and powerful reason for the great success the Refuge has experienced in helping men discover lasting deliverance over their addictions. Born out of his own addiction, Tom Thompson shares how God takes the brokenness of our lives and transforms it into a beautiful trophy of His love and grace through this thirteen-month Christ-centered residency program.

—Mark Fuller

Pastor, Grove City Church of the Nazarene

A Place of Refuge *is a transparent account of Tom's hard journey from a destructive lifestyle to being an effective leader of a ministry that is rebuilding broken lives. The book is filled with penetrating insights and wise advice for anyone currently in leadership or considering starting a ministry. You will be inspired by the testimonies of changed lives and challenged to fully devote yourself to the calling God has for your life.*

—Tyler Flynn

Executive Director, Mission Columbus

A Place of Refuge *is a high-value read. It is an autobiography of a gifted leader, an inspiration for those looking for their calling, and a blueprint for a process of transforming lives. Wisdom comes with time, trials, error, and success, and Tom has experienced it all and openly and honestly shares his experiences. This is a must-read for both those in ministry and those considering a ministry calling.*

—Dan Gregory
Business Development Consultant

This is a timely book for a lot of people—you included! Having watched the extraordinary personal journey of my friend Tom Thompson and seeing the development of the Refuge over the years, I am excited that he has shared this journey with the world. I am excited for you to read this book and share the journey with hundreds of other people. Read this book and then write a few chapters of your own!

—Mark W. Pfeifer
Lead Pastor, Open Door Church,
Chillicothe, Ohio

A PLACE
of
REFUGE

A PLACE *of* REFUGE

A CALL FROM GOD TO SERVE OTHERS

TOM THOMPSON

Printed in the United States of America

Library of Congress Control Number: 2017958096

ISBN Paperback: 978-1-947368-17-0
ISBN eBook: 978-1-947368-35-4

Cover Design: eventart
Interior Design: Ghislain Viau

To Johna

Contents

PART 3 - Time to Write Your Story

Acknowledgements

This book is dedicated to my wife, Johna. Without her love and support, I would not be where I am today. Her strength and constant presence in my life nurtured me when I had no strength of my own. She followed me when I wouldn't have. She has served me and forgiven me with a Christ-centered heart and soul. She is the backbone of our family and provides an example of living in the name and teachings of Jesus, and I am forever grateful. Thank you.

Thank you also to my family—Wes, Amber, Stella, Trent, Luke, and Logan. God has blessed me beyond measure with your presence and love. Thank you to my parents, who taught me love and commitment by their example to one another through the years. Many thanks as well to my in-laws, John and Mary, who supported our family through the lean and good times through their generosity and unconditional love.

This book is also dedicated to the servants whom God has designated as His vessels to serve and volunteer their time, talent, and resources to the people who have no voice. The Refuge has been built by an army of God. I have experienced the presence of Jesus by watching His people carry out his wishes. They have kept me in the war by their examples throughout the years. Though there are too many to mention by name, all of them are a picture of One, and His name is Jesus Christ.

Most of all, I thank my heavenly Father who has shown me unconditional love, total acceptance, and grace beyond comprehension. I thank Him for accepting me and all my imperfections.

Foreword

Tom Thompson is a man of faith, grit, and determination. Many talk about faith, but as the writer of the Book of James tells us, faith without works is dead. God gave Pastor Tom Thompson a vision, and with a courageous faith, he acted upon the promptings that continually unfold even today into the greatest adventure of his life and that of his family. He and his wife, Johna, have a beautiful family, but they have also birthed a timely ministry that is not only vital to the kingdom of God but crucial for the cultural epidemic our country and communities now face. When God began to lay out the vision for Tom, little did he know that this grassroots ministry called the Refuge would touch the lives of countless thousands of men and their families around the globe.

The Refuge is a spiritual boot camp that impacts mens' lives with a spiritual foundation that instills in them the skills for living a life that makes a difference on every level. This is a book of the faith and courage of one man and his family. It's a testament of how Tom's deliverance from addiction would later lead to freedom for countless others. It's a story of fear, pain, struggle, and lack. It's also a book of faith, peace, success, and conquering. It's a story that proves that one man's faith and the courage to act upon that faith have ultimately led to life change for countless men and their families through a spirit-led, heartfelt organization that is all about being empowered to serve others through a ministry called the Refuge. The Refuge is just that; it is a refuge for the hurting and broken so they can be set free and empowered to live lives of freedom that will ultimately lead to life change for others. This book will bless you and encourage you. But most of all it will stir your faith and challenge you to believe in more while becoming all God intended for you to be.

—Rob Collins
Pastor, Calvary Memorial Church
Parkersburg, West Virginia

A Note from the Author

This book chronicles the transformative personal and spiritual journey that led me to establish the Refuge, a Christ-centered rehabilitation center for men addicted to drugs and alcohol, and grow what was once merely a vision into the small but thriving community that it has become today. This journey has lasted more than two decades now, from conception to establishment to the current growth phase.

Along the way, many people have asked me about my journey. I knew it was a story worth telling, and I did so in an informal fashion, but it is only now, with twenty years of reflection, that I have found the courage and clarity of thought to put pen to paper and do the story justice. For the longest time, I hesitated to write this book. I was afraid my story, in book form, would sound boastful or self-aggrandizing, which is never what the Refuge has been about. I founded the Refuge to help broken men heal, learn to walk with God, and find their true calling. It was never about me. Everything I have done and will ever do is in the name of God.

I realized that not only could I tell my story, I *had* to tell my story. God uses our weakest and darkest moments in service of His own holy work. This book is a reflection of that truth. I myself was once a broken man. Through refinding Christ, I was not only healed, but found my true calling in life. That is a story worth telling because it honors God and reveals the awesome healing and corrective power of His word and work.

My hope for this book is that it will mirror the work I do at the Refuge. I hope this book will help you find the strength, fortitude, and perseverance to achieve your higher purpose, even when the road ahead seems blocked by all kinds of insurmountable obstacles, even when your faith feels tested, even when you aren't sure what path your life should take.

This book is divided into three parts. Part 1 tells my personal story and that of the Refuge. It covers how I found myself a broken man, rediscovered God's full role in my life, and healed myself by rededicating my life to serving God and His children.

Part 2 details the inner workings of the Refuge and the work that we do there. Those readers interested in starting ministries and organizations similar to the Refuge will find the foundational framework to get started here. I hope that all people, whether their calling aligns with mine or not, find this section inspiring and that it will lead them to seek the same excellence and purity of service in their own work.

Part 3 of this book is meant to help readers find their true calling in life. Maybe it is to found a ministry like the Refuge. Maybe it is something different. Either way, I hope this section helps you find and better articulate your true calling so that you can start making it a reality.

Finally, the book concludes with a call to action—to start making your calling and your life one and the same.

PART 1

Birth of the Refuge and My Story

CHAPTER 1

Heeding the Call: Off the Interstate and onto God's Path

I was on Interstate 270 in Ohio, headed to Zanesville from Columbus, when God gave me my life's calling. The vision struck me with such power that I had to pull over onto the shoulder to avoid an accident as cars were flying by. I sat there, rocking slightly, touching my forehead. My eyes struggled to focus. My ears were ringing. I was literally in tears over what God had shown me.

The vision was lucid and crisp, practically real enough for me to reach out and touch. I saw a farm. It was a safe place, far from the hustle and bustle of the city—a sanctuary tucked away in the sprawling open country of America's heartland.

This was a rural place steeped in pastoral beauty and simplicity.

This was not simply a farm. It was a ministry in the woods. The people there were those most in need of such a place. They were broken men who had come to the country to find tranquility and start healing.

They had come not only to find Jesus, but also to find themselves. This was a place where the troubled could come and simply *be*. Above all, my vision was of a place where people could escape their lives so that they might learn how to live. They would be able to distance themselves from the situations and circumstances that were keeping them in a bad place. They would step away from broken lives, broken relationships, and the shame and guilt that had kept them in a cycle of failure. The place He was showing me was no mere farm—nor was it a halfway house or social program. The place He was showing me was a ministry of sorts. It was a sanctuary where men could come and practice worship and servitude. It was a place where one could receive His unconditional love and His acceptance. It was a place where all could simply be part of His creation and not have to worry about the problems and brokenness that had marred their lives.

This vision was no hallucination; it was palpable and real. I knew in my heart that it was a message straight from our Lord in Heaven. The voice of God was filling up my spirit and showing this place to me. My heart knew His voice.

Deep down, I knew almost immediately that the Lord was calling me to do His work by making this vision a reality.

Why had God shown *me* this vision? At that point, I did not know why God had specifically selected me to do this work, but I did have firsthand knowledge of the type of men who needed such a place. Years earlier, not so long before this vision, I had been one such man: broken, and an alcoholic. I had been a man with no hope for himself or the future. Many times, I had found myself on the brink of suicide before pulling myself back from the abyss.

Perhaps this is the reason God called upon me. Maybe my trials and tribulations, my own struggles with brokenness and addiction, were mere preparation for this calling. I will never know, but in the end, it doesn't matter.

Whatever the reason, His voice was clear. The Lord was saying to me, "You are My son. Everyone is My child, and needs a place to just *be*." The men in my vision needed this place, and He was asking me to build it.

While this vision had been utterly overwhelming, the experience had also given me a total sense of peace in this world. A near-smothering calm had descended over me. I was shaken to my core—but I knew that everything was going to be OK. It turned out that it would be even better than OK. After I had struggled for years to find my purpose in life, God had finally given it to me. This is the reason I felt such serenity.

For most of my life, especially the prior decade, I had wanted so much to do the Lord's work. Long ago I learned that, in the end, there is no one in this world to please except for our Lord. I am not here to please others—not my family nor my community. I *serve* both, but I do so to please God. Only in this way does one find peace.

This mode of thinking has allowed me to correct my course and finally get on the right track in life. But it has taken me a long time to get here. I had spent much of my life saddled with and paralyzed by other people's expectations. I had wanted to please everyone. I'd wanted to be loved and liked, and to be what other people needed so that I might gain validation and respect.

This was a trap. Sometimes I came up short of other people's expectations. This sent me into a spiral of guilt and shame. Failure crippled and paralyzed me. Failure sent me back to the bottle and, ultimately, right back to the bottom. I would then claw my way back up to the surface, only to repeat the cycle yet again.

I was only able to break this cycle by freeing myself of the expectations of others. This truth took me a long time to learn, because I was so entrenched in the busyness of living in my own small world. My own life was a distraction from my true purpose: serving God.

But what if I'd had access to a place totally free of people and their expectations? What if I had been able to escape my own life long enough to heal and find a relationship with God? What if I had been able to bypass all the shame and guilt by escaping from my own life for a short time?

The answer is that such a reprieve, such a place, would have allowed me to begin thriving much sooner. It was just such a place that God was showing me as I sat in my car on the side of the freeway.

A Place of One's Own

This vision did not arrive out of nowhere; I had been speaking to God when it came. While driving on the interstate that day, I was thinking about two men I had known in my Promise Keepers group.

Like many of us, they had been drawn to the group because they were broken. These men were also addicted. I believe that God heard my thoughts and prayers about these men and that the vision was, in part, His answer to a problem that continues to plague the broken and the addicted: they often have nowhere to go to find themselves. God's answer was the refuge in my vision.

Promise Keepers is a Christ-centered, nationwide organization dedicated to helping men lead better lives by accepting Jesus Christ as their Lord and Savior and holding each other accountable to be godly husbands and fathers. The movement emerged in the early 1990s and quickly became very popular. The organization held large events that would fill stadiums. While these were impactful events, they weren't as powerful as the small group meetings held in community spaces, churches, and homes.

I hosted one such Promise Keepers group in my basement for several years.

This group was central to helping me get my life back on track. The members gave me community when I'd had none.

They held me accountable and helped me hold myself accountable. I had already joined Alcoholics Anonymous and worked the Twelve Steps. I had a relationship with Jesus Christ and I was sober by that time, but I was still coming out of my "dry drunk" phase. I needed community to keep me accountable, and I found it in Promise Keepers.

We were a tight-knit group. During our weekly discussion groups in my basement, we poured out our hearts and souls to each other. We shared. We cried. We trusted one another and kept each others' secrets. Our spiritual lives became entangled for those brief hours during which we got to know each other very well.

In addition to the meetings in my basement, we also attended some of the larger Promise Keeper events. These were inspiring trips that took us out on the road together, usually carpooling in a big van. Members of the group would sometimes invite guests as a way to introduce others to Promise Keepers. These events could be a powerful crash course.

We once had a member invite two men with us to an event in Pontiac, Michigan. At the time, they were both struggling with personal issues, including drinking problems and marital troubles. We didn't know them, as they neither attended the church nor any of the groups that we did, but we knew their issues well. Our whole group was dedicated to helping each other overcome these problems. They were perfect candidates for Promise Keepers and had much to gain. With open arms and hearts, we welcomed them to carpool with us on the trip.

As it turned out, their interest in joining us wasn't entirely spiritual. Neither of them was religious, and they just wanted to ride along with their friend and check out the event. We were a little afraid they would just goof off the whole time and take advantage of the trip.

This couldn't have been further from the truth. They were both floored by what they saw at the Promise Keepers event. They were delighted by the sense of community and utterly rapt by the speakers. They loved the positive energy and saw value in the ideas put forward about what it meant to be a good and accountable man.

We talked with them a lot on the way home, sharing stories in the van and over meals. Afterward, they began coming to our weekly group. It was exciting to see them become so engaged. They really wanted to change and grow and heal.

Unfortunately, it didn't last.

They began to slip not long after having returned home. The talks in Michigan had energized them. They had loved the sense of community that talking to and spending time with us on the road had given them. They had our support, and we could hold them accountable, but returning home meant returning to their lives and all their problems.

We started to lose touch with them as they attended fewer and fewer meetings. We all resided in the Columbus suburbs, but they were farther away. Without anyone to hold them accountable, they started backsliding. They returned to heavy drinking, continued to have marital problems, and succumbed to the same cycle of failure, guilt, and shame that had plagued me for years.

They eventually stopped showing up to meetings altogether, which was very disappointing to the members of our group. We had invested a lot of time and energy into helping them through their issues, and it now felt like a sad waste. I didn't regret *trying* to reach out and help them; I regretted that we had ultimately *failed*. I was frustrated with these two men, but I was much more frustrated by our own inability to help them.

It was these two men I was thinking about while driving down Interstate 270 that one fateful day. I was utterly exasperated just thinking about the two men. My anger started to get the better of me. I wanted to help people; that was why I was so involved with Promise Keepers. But what was the point if we were only going to lose touch? What was the purpose of helping people do better if they were just going to backslide?

Their failure, and the failure of men like them, rocked me to the core and tested my faith in my own generosity. I started to wonder if anyone could ever really help anyone. It felt like people had to save themselves, and there was nothing we could do for anyone.

Even then I recognized those thoughts as toxic. Rather than let the thoughts continue to consume me, I turned to God and talked with Him. Right there in my car, barreling down the freeway, I asked Him, "Why even help anybody?

What is the point? Can I really do any good? How can I help change a person's life if he's simply going to return to the same life, the same circumstances, that he has been struggling with all along?"

This was a humbling experience. I was ashamed to stand before God and pose these questions. I had wanted to help, but doing so seemed impossible. I felt at a total loss.

This is when I had the vision, hit the brakes, and pulled over to the side of the road. The farm appeared so very vividly in my mind and heart, and I heard the voice of God. I'd had a question, and He provided the answer: you can help someone escape his life by *literally* helping him escape his life.

The two men with whom we had lost touch could have benefited from a place like the one God showed me. They had thrived when they were alone and on the road with us. But they failed to overcome their own situations. Returning to their homes, their communities, and their broken lives too early had proved too detrimental, too much to overcome, and too much of an obstacle for them to continue to walk the narrow path.

But if they had been given a place where they could sequester themselves with people working through similar problems and focus on nothing but themselves and their relationship with God, they might have been able to reach escape velocity. Their own broken lives had pulled them back down to Earth. But what if they were *physically* removed from their lives while they worked through their problems?

I already knew the answer, as I had lived this same problem. God simply held up a mirror for me. He reminded me how hard it had been for me to escape my own poor choices and negative thoughts. I had gone back to drinking many times before I could overcome my own shame and guilt. It had taken me years to escape my life.

But what would have happened if I had been provided with a place to work through my problems *before* returning to work, my family, my community, and all the problems that had come to define my life?

I was floored, and in tears. I saw a simple way to make the world a better place for those who are suffering.

I now had the answer to a question that had been plaguing me for quite some time. God had shown the me the answer. I didn't know what to do with that answer, or how to make the vision a reality, but the answer was there, plain as day.

By this point in my life, I had already overcome many of my own personal demons. I had a strong and active relationship with my Lord. I felt accepted by God. I felt totally OK with who I was.

What I had come to realize now, through the vision, was that God wanted this for everyone. He wanted me to share the peace He had helped me attain. He wanted me to share it with others, far and wide.

His message was this: I couldn't *give* them peace. But I could create a place where broken men could more easily find Him and, by proxy, find themselves.

Onto God's Path

My vision shook me; I was literally trembling when I returned home that day. I was nervous and excited all at the same time. The vision was beautiful, but if it was truly the Lord calling upon me, it came with tremendous responsibility. I didn't even know where to begin. How was I to make the vision a reality?

I immediately went home and shared the experience with my wife. I was surprised because she listened with an open heart and didn't think I was crazy. We both agreed that it was all about God's timing. When did He want to bring this refuge to pass? God wanted me to build this place, which I would do, but *how*? I simply didn't know at that point, but I was resolved to find a way. I would make His vision a reality. I would make it my life's work to do His work. This is what it means to live a Christian life. Simply going to church and giving to charity are trappings, mere manifestations of this key principle of a faithful life. The faithful have faith and serve the Lord.

I spent the next few days and weeks thinking about what God had shown me. This was not a moment of soul searching, but rather, the beginning of a long spiritual journey and ongoing conversation with God. I was trying to hash out a plan in conversation with Him.

I first met with our pastors and other trusted friends to get their reaction. All of them were supportive. I then took the idea to my Promise Keepers group. I talked to people there about what good such a place could accomplish. We discussed how such a place could have helped us in our own lives. I wanted to gauge people's interest in a place like the one I had seen in my vision.

I was just putting out feelers, gauging interest and reactions, and trying to think about how I could make my vision a reality. I didn't have a grand plan, and I was riddled with doubt and insecurity. I did not at all know how I would make this happen.

We heard of a similar farm in Illinois, so a close friend and I went to visit this farm to see how they did things. I spoke with leaders and pastors in our city to see what else was available in our community and to see what I could learn. I made many phone calls and met with dozens of people.

Within a year, I was selling my house, my business, and some of our possessions. I was getting rid of everything we owned and uprooting my whole family. In order to create something more, we were giving up the comfortable lives we had once fought so hard to build. We were ready to embark on a journey of faith to create this place God had shown me. It was a journey not just for me but my whole family; I had a wife and four sons who would be affected by this. Of course, my wife and I had been praying fervently for months about all of this, but what about our children? I met with my oldest son to explain what our family was about to do. To ask him how he felt about it. He was in the sixth grade at the time. We prayed together about it. Our children seemed to understand and accept the change. And, to my delight, people began to rally around me in surprising ways. I didn't have a plan; I just needed faith and a willingness to sacrifice and serve.

I will touch on the specifics of how this happened later in this book, as well as explain how *you* can step up and rally the resources of your church and community to create a similar movement of your own. That is the whole purpose of this book: to inspire people with my story so that they too may take up the Lord's work and create positive change in servitude to others.

But, for now, I will tell you that this is how it all started—with a calling. This wasn't something I had created in my mind. I was merely a conduit—the antenna—the same as all of us who are ready to receive God's signal. The reception couldn't have been clearer, louder, or more powerful. It had wedged itself into my every waking thought.

Now I just needed to act, to step out in faith. I didn't yet know how to do so, only that I *had* to. I had to lift my foot and take the first step. My hope for this book is that it inspires others to do the same.

CHAPTER 2

Starting the Refuge: Faith and Sacrifice

While God's vision to provide a place where men could receive God's unconditional love, away from the distractions of the city, was clear, He had provided no blueprint. He had shown me the path, but the way was not lit. He was not holding my hand. It was up to me to fill in the blanks and figure out how to do His work. I had been given the vision, but it was up to me to come up with a plan and make that vision a reality.

I don't know why God chose me. It certainly wasn't a result of any professional expertise on my part. I was a businessman who worked in sales, so I knew how to start a business. My knowledge of running a farm was best described as nonexistent. The idea of me, a salesman from the suburbs, as a farmer was laughable! I did have experience running a small business. But

I was certainly not an addiction specialist, nor a minister of any type. I had never run a nonprofit or a social program. I was, by all appearances, in over my head.

My most relevant experience was running my Promise Keepers group. But that had been a small, meet-up group based around a national movement that had provided its own materials, model, and methods. With the Refuge, I was starting from scratch. I had to build the organization from the ground up. There were important decisions to be made in areas in which I had no personal experience or expertise.

Practically speaking, I didn't know the first thing about starting a place like the one I had envisioned. But I had faith. I was willing to learn and make personal sacrifices. In the end, this is what mattered most.

The True Meaning of Self-Sacrifice

The sacrifices would be made by my entire family. We had to deal with financial hurdles right from the start. God was asking us to buy a farm and build facilities to accommodate people while they healed. We needed land, housing, and community spaces for worship and meetings. Staff was just another thing needed.

We weren't even sure we would be able to find people to serve! What if we opened and no one showed up? What if no one even wanted our services? People struggling with addictions might benefit from leaving behind their troubled lives, but that was no guarantee they would do so. Ultimately, these worries were not helpful. There were many things that had to be done and built before we could even begin offering services.

We focused first on coming up with a financial plan. None of this would be cheap, yet from the very start, we were short on money.

I was willing to make sacrifices to get this off the ground, including putting up my family's savings. I was even willing to sell our house and use some of the money to buy the farm. I wanted to sink every penny into this God-sized vision, but it still wouldn't have been enough. We would come up short, even once the house sold and our retirement accounts were empty. This was a hard truth to confront. Being unable to afford to heed God's call was the most bitter pill I had ever known. It was also one I refused to swallow.

I put my faith in God and started looking for a place to build the Refuge before we even had the money to pay for everything. I didn't know how I would afford to heed God's call, just that the price of *not* doing so was too high. I felt like I had no other choice but to move forward with faith—blind faith, if necessary.

This is the reason we were willing to make sacrifices, and sacrifice we did. I was thirty-five years old when God gave me this calling, and my wife was thirty-six. Things had been going well for us. We had built comfortable lives for ourselves. I was working in scholastic sales, selling materials to high schools, while my wife worked for the state. Our cushy jobs afforded us ample free time and financial security. We were blessed to be able to send our four beautiful children to a private Christian school. We were in the best financial shape of our lives and had finally achieved happiness after many years of marital strife and financial problems. I had battled depression and alcoholism, and I was winning. I had finally become the husband and provider I should have been from the start.

We had pushed through some very dark years and had finally found ourselves happy and comfortable on the other side. We were more than just "making it"; we were blessed. We had achieved the great American Dream.

Following God's path meant putting all that comfort and personal happiness on the line. Walking down His path meant walking away from all that we had achieved for ourselves. God had called upon me to build a refuge for the broken. Heeding His call meant forfeiting all the security and comfort we had worked so hard to attain. We were no longer working for ourselves; we were working for Him now. Every penny we made would have to go toward our mission. We wouldn't be able to buy the best new gadgets and luxuries. Instead, we would have to pinch every penny and then tighten our belts even more. This was not an easy decision to make, but in the end, I knew what I had to do. For me, life became about serving the Lord.

This was a true leap of faith. There were no guarantees of success, and no certainties. I saw the path before us, but knew not where it would take us, only that we had to walk it. We might fail; we might not. There was no way to know.

In the end, it didn't matter. We would take the first step and then the next. We would make the journey. God had spoken and His vision was clear: He wanted me to build this place. The only thing that mattered to me was heeding His call. We were not waiting for a paycheck or weighing life's options. We were just doing the work.

Buying the Farm—A Big Leap of Faith

Before we could start the Refuge on a farm, we needed to buy the land. I barely knew a farm from a ranch. I knew even less about obtaining agricultural zoning—not that we have ever actually raised crops—than I did about obtaining 501(c)(3) nonprofit status. I certainly didn't know about choosing the right location, much less how to pay for the land.

I didn't need to know these things to just get started. I rolled up my sleeves and got ready to sweat. With no practical experience, I simply put my faith in God. I followed the path He laid before me and prayed for Him to deliver the way.

Of course, the Lord delivered; He always does. He laid out the path, while all I had to do was listen and follow. Every time I was unsure about something, I listened carefully to those around me, to my heart, and to signs from God. This carried us through when we didn't know where to turn.

For example, we didn't know what part of the country we should choose for the Refuge. The answer presented itself when I was visiting a childhood friend in Chillicothe, Ohio. His father was a pastor at the church where I first got saved.

We had fallen out of touch, but now that I had found God again and was reconnected with the Word and my spirituality, we had rekindled our friendship.

He was now a pastor, just like his father. I attended one of his services and watched him preach. The night before, we had talked about how I wanted to build a refuge for men struggling with addiction. He thought the idea was a great one and brought it up during his sermon.

From the pulpit, he said, "My buddy Tom over here wants to start a place away from everything for men struggling with drugs and alcohol. Somewhere like, say, Vinton County."

Something clicked inside of me. I could almost hear a key turn. *Vinton County.* I had never heard of the place, but something told me this might be the place I had been praying about. I didn't even know where Vinton County was on the map. After the sermon, I talked to my friend about Vinton County. It was in a rural part of Appalachia, just east of Chillicothe. It sounded like the perfect place for men from Columbus and Cleveland and the other nearby cities to escape their lives.

When I got home, I studied up a little bit, did some reading, and became convinced that the Lord was pushing me to consider this place. I planned a trip to visit Vinton County and look around.

I showed up in my car with no itinerary, no plans, and only a vague idea of why I was there. There weren't any meetings scheduled. I didn't know anyone there. I just arrived and began striking up conversations with the locals.

This proved effective. The people of Vinton Country welcomed me with smiles and open arms. I was only there for a single afternoon but managed to meet many people who were willing to talk and offer advice. There was a realtor, a pastor, a municipal official at the courthouse, and a few other locals.

Unbeknownst to me at the time, many of these people would become instrumental to the process of getting the Refuge off the ground. All I knew was that they were kind and helpful. They listened to my story and they offered positive feedback and encouragement. They gave me insights I could not have gleaned without them. They helped convince me that this was the place.

The realtor was of immediate importance. She asked why I had picked Vinton County. I told her that my pastor friend had recommended it. I explained that since it felt like God was pushing me to this place, I had felt compelled to at least come and check it out.

"It just feels like the right place to buy land for something like this," I said. She laughed. "Well, you're definitely not from around here."

Genuine concern bled through her smile. She told me that it would be difficult to buy large plots of land in Vinton County for residence. The local people were mostly poor. The only thing they had to pass down to their children was their property. Land rarely went up on the market. I said that I would need at least a hundred acres.

"It's not really feasible to buy a hundred acres here," she said.

As important as this was for me to hear, I felt like my dreams had been dashed. I returned home discouraged. Maybe Vinton County wasn't the right place after all. But I had felt so sure. I went to bed feeling unsure.

There was a message waiting for me on the answering machine in the morning. I hit play and listened while making my morning coffee. The message was from the realtor.

"Mr. Thompson, I need you to call me back *immediately*. A couple came in last night after you left. They have some health problems and need to sell their place quickly. It's about 108 acres. It would be *perfect* for your purposes. I'm afraid to share it with anybody else. It will go quickly. They're putting it on the market soon. I've already got people that I know will buy it, but if you can get down here, we'll show it to you first. I don't know how long we can hold it for you, so you'd better hurry."

There were people anxious to see the property, but we were going to get first dibs. I was shocked. I was humbled. She was saving the lead for us. This stranger was putting me first, above the locals, because she believed in our mission. This was quite validating. We hadn't even gotten off the ground, hadn't even really gotten started, and already people believed in what we were doing. This was much-needed validation that helped to allay some of my concerns about comments expressed by a few persons who thought we were crazy.

I called her back, told her I was on my way, and rushed back to Vinton County that same day.

The relator took me to meet the sellers and see the land. The property was beautiful. I felt a sense of calm just walking the fields. The farm was everything I wanted—or at least I *thought* it was. I wasn't sure how much land we needed. Maybe this was too big. Maybe it wasn't big enough. I had no experience opening a ministry, no experience running a nonprofit, no experience working at a rehab, and certainly no experience managing a farm. I worried that making the wrong choice now would mean that the refuge I wanted to build would never come to be.

I knew from shopping around that the price was good, but it was still a lot of money—money we didn't even have. A mistake could sink us before we ever left port. We were selling our house and business to help pay for the farm, but the house hadn't sold yet. We needed the money now, and we didn't have cash in hand.

There wasn't much time for deliberation, but I needed a few minutes to think it over. Even though people were literally in line to see the place as I drove up to the house, I needed to be with God.

I walked down to a nearby stream called Raccoon Creek. It was a beautiful May day with spring about to give way to summer. The sun was shining. I walked down by the water, closed my eyes, and began to pray.

I asked God whether this was the right place. My gut told me this was the right path, but I was overcome with self-doubt, afraid of making the wrong decision. Some people had been warning me not to follow through with the whole thing. They told me not to throw my life away on some vague vision. They urged me not to buy a farm out in the middle of nowhere, in one of the most impoverished counties in Ohio, to serve people who, quite frankly, might not even be interested in our services. Some people felt it was too risky, that it was foolish.

Then it hit me. I wasn't simply scared of buying the wrong land; I was scared of following through at all. My heart was faltering.

"Lord," I said, eyes still closed, "I need Your guidance now. They're asking me to sign the contract. Should I buy this place?"

I opened my eyes and saw that a butterfly had started encircling me. After a moment, it was joined by another, and then another, and another. Suddenly, hundreds of butterflies were fluttering around me.

I can't prove it, and skeptics will dismiss this as coincidence, but in my heart, I knew this was a sign from God. It was a small, private miracle. God was telling me not to falter. He was telling me to make the deal.

I marched back to the farm with a new resolution. I had been gone maybe twenty minutes.

I then called my wife, who had been unable to come with me because one of our kids was sick. I explained to her how beautiful the farm was and my experience with the butterflies. I asked her whether I should make an offer. She did not hesitate and said we will just keep walking through these doors until they close. Make the offer and we will do our best to come up with the down payment. We agreed together to make an offer on the farm.

"Let's do it," I said.

We shook hands, and I signed the contract.

CHAPTER 3

You Don't Have to Go It Alone

We had thirty days to come up with the down payment. We only had a portion of the money in hand. The plan was to sell our house, but it hadn't gone on the market yet. There was no way we would sell the house and collect the money from the bank within thirty days. We would have to raise the money some other way.

This didn't stress me out as much as it maybe should have. I was putting full faith in God. The experience by the creek in Vinton County, the miracle with the butterflies, had instilled in me a new confidence. I truly believed that everything was going to be OK.

Throughout the history of the Refuge, we have depended on two things: God and community. These have been enough to carry us through. I had already turned to God for help and done all I could. Now it was time to lean on those around me.

At first, I had been reluctant to tell people about my vision and my plans. I was afraid they would think I was crazy. Self-doubt kept me silent for a while. Of course, I did have to tell the people close to me. I started with the person who was closest—my wife. As my life partner and the mother of my four children, she had to be on board for me to proceed. No one would have blamed her for not wanting to sell our house and move to the country to start a ministry for alcoholics and people addicted to drugs. I certainly wouldn't have blamed her. But I was certain that she would support me in the endeavor when she understood how important it was to me and that the calling was from God.

I explained my vision to her and told her I wanted to start a refuge like the one I had been shown by God. I was upfront and clear about what this would mean for our lives.

In essence, I was making my case, but I was not trying to persuade her. Her decision needed to be her own. It was important that she not consult only with me, but directly with God. I told her only what I had seen and thought, and then asked her to contemplate the decision for a while. She consulted with God, in her own heart, explaining things to Him from her point of view.

After mulling it over by herself and with God, she got back to me. She did not, of course, think that I was crazy. On the contrary, she was ready to go all in. She understood that this was important work and could see the signs pointing *both* of us in this direction. God was calling on us to make this journey together. This was simply an extension of the spiritual journey we had been on since first coming together in a biblical union.

She was convinced by many of the same signs that had convinced me. She had faith in my vision and could hear God speaking to both of us. She could see Him pushing me toward Vinton County.

These signs were numerous and consistent, and they were very important to us. We considered them confirmation from God, which we would continue to receive throughout the journey; the vision was just the beginning. Then came the unexpected discovery of Vinton County and the moment with the butterflies down by Raccoon Creek when I was starting to question my path. We experienced one small miracle after another. Every time our hearts began to stray, God gave us the strength and resolve to continue moving forward.

Another sign came during our garage sale when our house sold before we even put it up for sale. We were cleaning and thinning out our possessions in preparation for putting the house on the market. In the back of the garage, I had a "For Sale by Owner" sign that I hadn't yet had a chance to put up in the yard. A man at the garage sale saw the sign from the road and asked, "The house is for sale?"

"It sure is," I replied.

He asked if he could see it first before we put the sign out. We said sure. He came to see it three times before making an offer.

The house sold before we even listed it, giving us the financial cushion and personal freedom we needed to start making big moves toward opening the Refuge and moving to Vinton County.

These were only small moments that seemed to indicate that we were on the right path. I call these moments our "divine appointments." They gave us strength and courage and kept us going when things got difficult.

Thankfully, these divine appointments never ceased. We kept finding doors before us; all we had to do was open them and step through. We bought the farm in July of 1999, and almost two decades later, we are still going strong.

The clearest sign from God that we were on the right path was the fact that people kept rallying around us. Both sets of parents supported us by watching the kids and making donations as well. Our extended families started offering support. Some people offered their time or services. Others wrote checks to cover expenses. Members of my old Promise Keepers support group and people from church made early donations.

We took our message to everyone we knew. My greatest fear was that people would call us crazy. In fact, many people *did* think we were not thinking clearly. People called us all kinds of things once we started selling our possessions as we prepared to sell our house. But others were willing to volunteer and write checks. Some people who thought we were crazy wrote checks anyway!

The more the word got out, the more the donations of time and money poured in. We started to benefit from a snowball effect. More and more donors stepped forward. At first, support had been limited to our immediate sphere of influence. Eventually, we started receiving donations from people we had never met. Thousands of dollars rolled in, allowing us to buy the farm and start building the infrastructure we needed to accept the first people into the ministry.

I cannot stress this enough: People who want to start something like this may be daunted by the enormity of the task, but you must understand that **you do not have to go it alone**. Do good work, put your heart into your endeavor, stay true to the vision provided by God, and people will come together and help make your vision a reality.

You *don't* have to go it alone. In fact, you probably *can't* go it alone. Ambitious projects are seldom the work of one man. Creating great things takes whole communities coming together, making sacrifices, and working together. Reach out to your community. Trust them to help you.

From the start, and to this day, the Refuge has been a small organization funded primarily by small donations from the community. We are a true grassroots nonprofit. Individuals provide a portion of our funds: not foundations, not grants, not government programs. This allows us to do things our way, a biblical way. Some people have gifted us as much as $25,000 to build specific facilities and additions. But the majority of our funding comes from much smaller donations, as well as the work put in by the staff of the ministry, the men who work to help pay for their discipleship journey, and the partnering businesses that support the work we do.

We depended on God and community, and God and community came through for us. I cannot thank God enough for this success. I had prayed for everything to work out. Now I know God was listening to my prayers. He was answering them. He was showing me the way. He was bringing His called people to our aid.

There is no way I could have done this alone. Starting a nonprofit or business is difficult. You must invest time and money. I was happy to give both, and I was happy to make sacrifices.

But that wasn't enough. There wasn't enough time in the day for me to do everything myself, and we certainly didn't have the money. The investment required far exceeded my savings. We sacrificed our house and life savings, and it still wasn't all we needed to get the ministry running.

What we needed was for people to come together and help us build this thing, and that is exactly what happened. We have built a true community around the Refuge—one that has continued to grow and flourish for years now. It is made up of donors, volunteers, and staff, many of them the very men who came through the ministry. After getting their own lives together, they wanted to give back by contributing to the Refuge. Men who have come to the ministry utterly broken have gone on to fix their lives only to return and serve. They have joined the staff, and become givers and volunteers. They personally sacrifice for the Refuge by putting in blood, sweat, and tears when they can. Several of the people who work at the ministry have been with us for many years. We have a bond that runs deep because we are building something together through and for Christ.

As the founder, this gives me a great sense of satisfaction and validation. I can *see* that the Refuge is changing lives. I know this because those whose lives have been changed have come back to pay it forward and help the next man up. They believe so strongly in the ministry that they are willing to make sacrifices to help others. They saw how other people helped me help them, and now they want to help the Refuge help others.

I could never have imagined building such a positive and powerful force when I left my business, bought a farm in the country, and started the Refuge. I could never have conceived of such success.

Never had I dreamed of such a rewarding and fulfilling calling. I had come to this from a place of sacrifice—but it was a sacrifice that paid back dividends a hundredfold. The Refuge has never and will never make me financially wealthy. That was never the purpose. But it has made me rich in spirit, rich in friends, rich in community, and rich in a deeper relationship with God. For this, I am forever grateful. These men, many of them who came through the ministry, have sacrificed right there with me. It is a powerful bond.

I want the same thing for every man who comes through the ministry. I want them to forge lifetime bonds and form their own bands of brothers among our ranks. The relationships we have in life are what make it worth living. They nurture us and give us strength. And for those of us at the Refuge, they keep us sober and on God's path. I consider the people in my life not just a gift but also "The Gift." The people I have come to know through the Refuge are the greatest gift God has bestowed upon me. They have sacrificed time and money, and they have come together with me to build something amazing and glorifying to God.

I want this sense of fulfillment for everyone.

I want it for the men at the Refuge.

I want this for all God's sons and daughters.

I want this for *you*.

I want to help others do what I have done and build similar communities.

I didn't start the Refuge alone, and you don't have to either. If you believe in your vision, and it is a God-given one, and you put in the blood, sweat, and tears, then **other people will join you in your cause.** You just need to do the work, be willing to make sacrifices, believe in what you are doing, and remain true to the vision. When people see you making sacrifices and doing the work, they will want to make sacrifices and contributions in kind.

It worked for us, and it can work for you. Don't let lack of money get in the way. For that matter, don't let lack of expertise, manpower, resources, or anything else deter you from your calling in life. If you commit yourself to a worthy cause in God's will, then He and your community will deliver.

If there is one thing I learned in Alcoholics Anonymous, it was to take things one day at a time. I applied this same wisdom to running the Refuge. We didn't worry about the future, but we prayed constantly. We asked ourselves what we needed now and prayed about how to get it. This works. Every time a new expense came up, God provided the money. Not always in the timing we wanted, but we always had our needs met. We didn't always have the cash, or the people, or the land, or even the know-how. But in His timing and in His way, it would come to pass. Every single time, we found our way.

With time, things got easier, because our faith got stronger. Each success led to the next. When people learned that we were making it happen, things began to snowball. We located resources and financing. One day, many years after having thrown our whole lives into disarray, we looked around and rediscovered that God is amazing. We had a peaceful home life, our kids were doing well, and the Refuge was becoming not only a reality, but also a blessing to many.

We have been at it for years and now have three locations. We have served thirty-five hundred men in our long tenure and have expanded our ministries. Now we even host events, including pastor conferences to help fight heroin addiction. Our experience working with men with addictions has made us a trusted authority in the field, and we have become an asset to others who are working to stamp it out.

With seventy to eighty men in residence at the ministry at any one time, we have become a stable, biblical organization. The men receive hands-on job training with our partner businesses and land jobs after leaving the ministry. We also provide training and opportunities to help them get started on the path to homeownership. They come in broken; they leave healed. We help them work on and improve all aspects of their lives, from marriage to work to homeownership, and beyond.

What God has built is inspiring. It's miraculous. We started with nothing, except a calling—and through the grace of God and the support of our communities, we have built a stable, Christ-centered ministry that is changing lives every day.

It wasn't easy. We put in a lot of work and received a lot of help. We prayed nonstop and, in the end, we made it happen by God's grace.

CHAPTER 4

On Brokenness, Part 1: My Story of Addiction

The meaning of life for all people of faith is the same: to love God and to love others, which spurs you to do God's work. For Christians, these commandments are the ultimate plumb line for our journey. There are many ways to do the Lord's work. His creation has many layers of complexity and is in need of many types of services. He gives each of us a different calling, and it is our job to walk with Him to discover what that is.

I discovered that my calling is to help lift up alcoholics and others struggling with addiction and offer them discipleship. By doing so, I can help them recover and heal from their addiction and other problems.

I sometimes thought about being unqualified for such a calling. My degree is in business, not medicine or psychology.

I am not a social worker, and I have no formal training in addiction or rehabilitation. Prior to getting my feet wet with the Refuge, I had no experience working directly in the field. I learned everything on the job.

Regardless, we succeeded in building a Christ-centered addiction center and sanctuary. We are helping to fix lives every day. Here we are, nearly two decades later, still going strong, still growing. This is the result of a lot of hard work and the will of God. I may not have had the right formal training or education, but I did have a *calling*. I put my heart and soul into the Refuge, knowing it was what God wanted of me.

I was not passive in this process, and my calling was not random. While I lacked formal training, I did not enter into my mission blindly. I had experience in small-group ministry through Promise Keepers at a local church. Running an organization efficiently was a skill I possessed because of my own experience in business. I committed myself fully to the calling.

If I had to guess, though, these are not the reasons God gave me this calling. My most important qualification, excluding the practical ones mentioned above, was my firsthand knowledge of addiction. I grew up around alcoholism and spent some years drinking and drugging. My long recovery, complete with many false starts and failures, gave me a crash course in what works and what doesn't. Nothing could have prepared me to work with those dealing with addictions as effectively as having struggled with it myself.

I understand clearly the truth of addiction: It is not rooted in the substance itself, or even any innate moral failing, but in a deep and profound spiritual brokenness. Addiction is, virtually without fail, more symptom than disease. The disease is a spiritual brokenness that often manifests in bad behavior, such as substance abuse and taking advantage of people. The use of drugs and alcohol is simply a symptom of the underlying problem: a broken person in need of a rescue through Jesus Christ.

This is definitely *not* to say that drugs and alcohol are not a huge problem; they are. In fact, most people with addictions will find themselves unable to address their true problems without first getting sober. But, once sober, many alcoholics and people with drug addiction find their lives still broken. Alcoholics enter what is colloquially known as a "dry drunk" phase. They are no longer actively drinking, but they still feel bad in many of the same ways. They still act like people with addictions even after the chemicals have been removed. They still feel broken, and overwhelmed with grief and shame. The brokenness that preceded the actual addiction remains.

The journey of recovery doesn't end when we stop using. That is where it *begins*. True recovery requires first removing the chemicals and then addressing the underlying problem. That isn't easy; the chemicals are the coping mechanism. Once they are removed, the person must face the problems that caused him or her to start using in the first place.

As a man walking in freedom through Jesus Christ, I have firsthand knowledge. Drinking didn't break me, and quitting drinking wasn't what fixed me; I was broken long before I started drinking. I was already in a place of desperation. I drank because I felt bad and "less than." But the alcohol only made things worse. Drinking took me right up to the precipice. My life was not only utterly broken, it actually seemed irreparable. My problems became unmanageable, and every day was a struggle.

There was not a single area of my life unaffected by my brokenness. My marriage was on the rocks. I was a bad father. My career was floundering. Depression was a daily reality. I was still in my twenties, but my life already felt like it was over. I had no direction and saw no path forward.

I didn't even understand what was wrong with me. My problem looked like a "quarter-life crisis" that had me questioning everything in my life. The truth was far more dire: I was having a *spiritual* crisis.

Life by the Drop

My addiction story is not so different from those of others. Its specific contours are familiar. Like many people, I started drinking in college and my consumption progressed steadily over time. Eventually, I reached a point where my drinking— and my life—became unmanageable.

I started drinking for all the regular reasons—mainly boredom and unhappiness. These are normal feelings. You don't have to have a terrible life to feel broken. My family was middle class—not rich, not poor. We had a nice house and plenty of nutritious food; all our needs were met, as well as most of our wants. I had good parents who encouraged my siblings and me to succeed in life.

This encouragement was sometimes hard for me. My father was a school superintendent who had high standards for his children. He challenged us to succeed in school, but I found it hard to measure up. I felt inadequate as a young person, especially when compared to my oldest brother. He excelled in athletics, playing football in high school and then in college. He later served as a captain for Woody Hayes at The Ohio State University.

My parents were proud of my brother's achievements. My father and my uncles had all played college sports. They respected athleticism almost as much as academics. Since I wasn't the best student, I tried to follow in my brother's footsteps by trying my hand at sports. As only a somewhat above-average high school athlete, I eventually decided that sports was not my passion and I wouldn't pursue it in college.

Failure seemed to be the one constant in my life. I felt like a failure, utterly hopeless about the future before I ever got out of my teens. But I kept trying. Upon graduation, I joined the military to pay my way through college. I spent six years in the National Guard. My military career should have been a point of pride, but instead, my pursuit of perfectionism led me to think, if you are not the general of the army you failed.

It wasn't just my military service about which I had an inferiority complex. I second-guessed every single decision I ever made. All my choices felt like the wrong ones. In my eyes, I never measured up in the eyes of others. I felt inadequate in comparison to my siblings, my parents, and basically everyone around me. I thought of myself as the black sheep of the family, the family failure—a total joke. They didn't actually feel this way, but *I* certainly did. This extended to all other relationships in my life. I never felt good enough, not at home, not on the field, not in the military, not in school.

By college, this toxic mind-set had become deeply entrenched. It was a part of my sense of self. I didn't just think I was a failure; I was *sure* I was a failure. It felt like an unchangeable fact that I would always be a failure and nothing would ever work out. College seemed like a slow-motion catastrophe that would end in a big reveal that proved, once and for all, that I was a failure. This seemed obvious to me from day one. I enrolled at The Ohio State University as an engineering major, but couldn't hack it in math and science classes. I switched to a business major to find my niche—*any* niche, really, but didn't know what business school entailed and I didn't have a passion for business. I just thought it would be easier than engineering. I needed an easier track. I couldn't bear pursuing engineering only to fail out of school.

This was all so demoralizing that I slipped into a depression. It didn't seem like anything would ever change.

Then I found alcohol. I started drinking at parties and soon discovered the bar scene. But this was not normal social drinking; I often drank alone, too. I liked the way alcohol numbed my pain. At least while I was drinking, alcohol allowed me to stop feeling so bad about myself. I stopped feeling much of anything at all.

I was soon drinking almost every day and would miss some classes due to hangovers. Sometimes, I would go to the bar *instead* of class. I also experimented a bit with drugs. Thankfully, I never got heavily into drugs; they just seemed like a novelty. It was alcohol that really spoke to me. Drinking numbed me better than anything else. Alcohol allowed me to forget how terrible I felt about myself without ever having to change anything in my life. I was never happy, but I was comfortably numb. I muddled through college with mediocre grades.

Alcohol and Marital Stress

Addiction affects every aspect of an addicted person's life. Relationships often suffer tremendously, and this was certainly the case for me. I lost track of friends through an active process: I so hated myself that I cut people out of my life. Afraid they would become disgusted with my behavior and turn their backs on me, I beat them to the punch by becoming a recluse.

The relationship that suffered the most was the one most important to me. My wife paid dearly for my addiction. She quickly lost the man she had married and found herself in a union that did not resemble what we had promised each other on our wedding day.

We met during my sophomore year of college. In retrospect, I feel she should have never had anything to do with me. While she was a promising young student, I was already a total mess. The night we met, I was hanging out in front of my house—drunk and high, of course. Out of boredom and loneliness, I started waving at passing cars, hoping someone would stop and talk to me. Everyone blew by without even noticing. Finally, a car with two women inside stopped at a nearby stop sign. Since they had the windows down, I shouted a hello. For some reason, they pulled over to chat with me. The driver was celebrating her birthday, so they invited me to join them at a dance club.

I eagerly agreed to accompany them and got to talking with the passenger. I was already smitten. She was beautiful, smart, and in my mind, perfect. It felt easy to open up to her—maybe *too* easy. I was drunk and words just started tumbling out of my mouth. I found myself rambling about my insecurities and despair. The floodgates just opened and every worry and fear that came to mind was verbalized. These are not the type of thing you tell someone within an hour of your first meeting.

She was nice and listened, but she was clearly wary of getting mixed up in my problems. Basically, I had already blown it. I was drunk and wearing my insecurities on my sleeve. It was obvious that she liked me, but she was hesitant to get involved with someone who was clearly such a mess. Nevertheless, she gave me her phone number. She'd had no reason to pull over, no reason to invite me out, no reason to listen to me air my dirty laundry, and certainly no reason to give me her phone number, but, thankfully, she did just that.

Despite having given her number to me, she wouldn't agree to go on a date with me. We talked on the phone from time to time, but that was it. She took pity on me and wanted to offer support, but she was reluctant to get too involved.

It took a year for her to finally agree to an actual first date. From there, things moved quickly. Six months later, we were engaged. We walked down the aisle before I even graduated. This was largely due to my rushing the relationship, since I wanted to get married before she could discover the "real" me. I was afraid the relationship would fall apart when that happened, so I proposed in an attempt to seal the deal.

Neither of us grew up in a Christian home. However, when we became engaged we decided we wanted to have God in our marriage. We found a church on campus. We attended services weekly. We went to bible study classes. We also signed up for marital counseling with the pastor.

At the time, a lot of my thinking was messed up. I think I saw marriage and church as a way to give my life purpose. I was lost and adrift. Everything felt devoid of meaning. Both college and my military career were unfulfilling. I needed something meaningful to which I could devote myself, and I thought marriage and a family could be those things. In essence, I wanted her to save me by providing me with a reason to live. This is no way to enter into a union. It was totally unfair to her and not at all what she had signed up for. No one can "complete" another person; only God can do that. But I had no relationship with God at the time, and there was a hole in my heart. I wanted to plug that hole with our marriage.

I was devoting myself to her when I should have first devoted myself to God. I didn't understand this at the time since I wasn't aware of my spiritual brokenness. All I knew was that something was missing from my life. I didn't know, hadn't even suspected, that what was absent was a relationship with God.

The marriage seemed doomed from the start. I was not good husband material: I drank too much. I was depressed and irritable. I was quick to anger. I was reclusive and withdrawn. I wasn't good at sharing feelings or being honest. The only thing I had going for me was good intentions. I thought marriage would force me to be responsible, clean up my ways, and become a better person. I was aware that being a responsible husband and father precluded heavy drinking. I would be forced to give up alcohol, which I very much wanted to do.

Unfortunately, I did *not* give up drinking. We both graduated and I began my career. We bought a house and had our first child, but I kept right on drinking through all of it. My fresh start had turned out to be anything but. I had adopted all the trappings of adulthood without actually maturing.

Deep down, I never actually *felt* like an adult; something inside me was still broken. This is what kept me drinking heavily. Being out of college, this was no longer socially acceptable, so I did my best to hide my problem from others.

Of course, some people still knew. My life was in shambles. I was angry and depressed most of the time. Nothing made me happy—not my career, not my family, not my marriage. I fought with my wife constantly, which was always my fault, never hers. Our relationship was broken because I was broken. I felt dead inside, a hollowed-out husk of a man. There wasn't enough of me to give to her.

Rather than take responsibility for this, I began to resent my wife. I felt trapped in the marriage. When she became pregnant with our first child, my first thought was not a joyful one; I was angry with her. I felt deceived and believed she was trying to trap me in the marriage by "getting pregnant."

"What do you *mean* you're pregnant?" I shouted in horror.

This was extremely painful for her to hear. It was pure, twisted selfishness. I was supposed to be celebrating with her—not making accusations, but my thinking was sick and distorted. We had talked about it on many occasions, but now I felt trapped in a marriage that wasn't working. Divorce had been my out; I had believed that, no matter how bad things got, I could always just walk away. Well, not anymore. I could leave my wife, but there was no leaving a child.

It wasn't just my marriage that made me feel trapped; it was my entire life. My career was unfulfilling, but now I was stuck because I had a family to support. This was overwhelmingly heavy to me. I didn't want to provide for a family, as I could barely provide for myself. Having a child would get in the way of drinking. I would have to be responsible. I would have to succeed at my career. I would have to make something of myself, which only intensified my fear of failure.

I didn't want any of this. All I wanted was to feed my addiction. I thought I wanted to stop drinking—except I didn't *really* want to stop drinking. I wanted to remain numb. Having a child would get in the way of this.

With divorce effectively off the table, my escape button was gone. This took me to a dark place. There was only one other way out: suicide. Thoughts of death began to consume me. I dreamed about death each night, and at work, I *day*dreamed about death. I fantasized about shooting myself, and it seemed like a rational course of action. I was convinced that others would be better off without me around to ruin their lives, and I thought I'd be better off too. It seemed like a win-win plan.

My depression worsened over time, as did my drinking. Every day was misery. Pretending to be happy and functional was torturous. I put on a fake smile and forced my way through each workday. Coming home was a respite, yet I would then leave to drink and let out a sigh of relief. I could finally just "be myself." I didn't have to pretend to be better than I really was. I could just sit in a bar, drink alcohol, and forget about my problems. Not wanting to disappoint anyone, or myself, I pushed people away. I hated myself and assumed everyone else hated me too.

I felt like more of a fraud than ever before. It was like being two different people. During the day, I forced myself to go into the world and make a living. I struggled through feelings of inadequacy while trying to sell myself to people, as that's what you must do in the business world. But on the inside, I was hurting.

All of this was very hard on my wife. As the only person around me anymore, she bore the brunt of my bad behavior. When I got angry and lashed out, it was at her. Only she saw this side of me. Often, I would come home totally miserable and just dump everything on her. I was miserable and wanted to make everyone else miserable too. Her only crime was being there, and her only fault was having made the mistake of marrying me.

On a regular basis, she walked around on eggshells to avoid setting me off. It didn't work. I would get drunk and throw tantrums over nothing, shouting, yelling, and belittling her. In a fit of rage, I once hurled our Christmas tree down the stairs. This not only scared my wife, it also scared *me*. I had always hated myself. Now, I was horrified by myself. I didn't understand what I was becoming, but whatever it was, it was not good.

A chasm developed between us. We became cold and distant. We were now husband and wife in name only; we were barely even friends. We certainly didn't seem to like or love each other anymore. I couldn't blame her for that; I had become a monster.

I started to doubt the marriage was going to last. I would have to change to save it, but change felt impossible to me. I believed I needed to keep drinking or everything would fall apart.

So I reasoned that if I could not change, she should change. I wanted her to accept my brokenness and failures. But, of course, she couldn't do this. She couldn't accept the drinking and the depression and the rages. She couldn't accept our toxic relationship. From my twisted perspective, this was a failure on her part. She couldn't be what I *thought* I needed, and I began to resent her and our marriage more and more.

Uncomfortably Numb

My drinking got worse until, eventually, I was drinking almost every day. My body may not have ever been physically dependent upon alcohol—I never quit drinking long enough to find out—but I was psychologically addicted. I would endure anything to keep drinking. My life, career, and marriage were all suffering—and still I drank. No matter how bad things got, that first sip would start to numb me against the pain. It was that numbness that I was after—that all people with addictions are after. It is the desire to stay numb that keeps us addicted, even as things get worse and worse. The worse things get, the more we want to remain numb. This is the primary driver of addiction: people with addictions need their chemicals to remain numb.

The chemicals become the most important thing; they usurp all other needs. Remaining numb is priority number one; everything else comes second. This drives people living with addictions to do selfish things. They'll do anything to get their chemicals, even if it means hurting others, which they do all the time. Even just staying numb hurts loved ones because it deprives them of the addicted person's true self. As addiction progresses, former boundaries slide backward. Those with addictions become willing to do whatever it takes to obtain their chemicals and remain numb.

Inflicting all this pain leads to guilt and shame and the need for more chemicals. This creates a vicious cycle in which people do increasingly abhorrent things to stay numb. This, in turn, exacerbates the need to stay numb and drives the addiction.

This is what happened to me. I drank because I was miserable, and I was miserable because I drank. I was trying to numb myself with alcohol, but the alcohol only made things worse. Drinking made me behave in terrible ways that induced guilt and shame. I would get drunk and act out. I would get drunk and go into rages. These things embarrassed and shamed me. The worse I behaved, the more I needed to numb myself.

This is a difficult cycle to escape. It is why people keep using even while their lives fall apart around them. My life was a disaster, but I didn't want to think about that. The only thing I would think about was drinking so that I didn't have to think about anything else.

It's Not (Just) the Chemicals—
Lessons from a Dry Drunk

This cycle had me feeling terrible all the time. I knew it had to end or it would end me. My wife was suffering. My family was suffering. I was suffering. Alcohol was a problem

I could no longer handle. My pain had become so intense that I could no longer fully numb myself against it. I had reached "my bottom," and I made the decision that I would quit drinking "cold turkey." I joined Alcoholics Anonymous and other support groups, and finally stopped drinking.

This may sound like a success, and in a way, it was. But sobriety didn't bring about the change I had hoped for. I had recognized that alcohol was causing me problems and cut it out of my life. But, to my surprise, I still felt bad. My wife told me things seemed worse since I stopped drinking. She noticed my rage and anger had increased. She was scared because she thought sobriety was the answer. She began reading books and getting help herself to understand how to deal with me. But I was still depressed and struggling with the issues that had driven me to drink in the first place. Despite sobriety, I remained unfulfilled. My business wasn't making me happy. My marriage wasn't fulfilling. Having a family wasn't enough. I still felt hollow and dead inside. I was depressed and I hated myself.

In fact, my depression actually felt *worse* once I got sober. Sobriety meant that I could no longer drink my problems away. I couldn't just numb myself to everything. I had to face my issues head on without alcohol as a crutch. This was difficult for me. I no longer had alcohol to blame for all my problems; my failures and shortcomings were now my own.

Sobriety wasn't the solution that I had expected. I was what twelve-step programs call a "dry drunk." I had given up the alcohol, but not the toxic thinking and behavior. Not actively drinking was an improvement, but no solution. I was surviving but certainly not thriving. Life still felt empty. I wasn't measuring up to my own expectations.

I became increasingly desperate for real solutions. I couldn't face being such a failure. If sobriety couldn't save me, what could? I started to doubt that I could ever be happy.

CHAPTER 5

On Brokenness, Part 2: My Story of Recovery

Sobriety did not fix my problems because alcohol was not my primary problem. Spiritual brokenness was my problem. Alcoholism was merely a symptom of that brokenness. I only drank because I had no sense of purpose in life. This made my life worse. Giving up the drinking was critical to my recovery, but I still lacked a sense of purpose even after I put the bottle down. I would not fully heal until I found truth and meaning in life, but I did not know where to even begin looking for these things.

Ultimately, I would not find truth and purpose until I found Jesus Christ. For me, there is no truth or purpose but God.

My life has been one long, winding path toward God. One of the first times I set foot in a church was at the age of sixteen. It was with a childhood friend whose father was a pastor—the same friend I mentioned in Chapter 2. It was a miraculous experience and an important day in my life.

During the altar call, the preacher walked up to the altar with several other people. I was just standing there, but I had my first real spiritual experience. Peace and love washed over my soul, and I was filled with hope. My body felt light, and my heart and soul were easy for perhaps the first time ever. I made the decision right then to start attending church on a regular basis.

I began going to Sunday services and learning about church and God. It was all very exciting at first, but I started to falter after a few months. The demands of the church were difficult for me. In my view at the time, this particular church was too focused on what one *shouldn't* do. This was incompatible with my errant ways. I was young and curious. The church was opposed to drinking, smoking, chasing girls, and basically everything that fills the minds of teenage boys who are on the wrong path in life. I wasn't supposed to even *think* about girls. Church began to seem less about spiritual fulfillment and more about controlling others with judgment and shame.

I wanted to be spiritual, but the Christian life presented to me by this church was all about the "dos" and the "don'ts" of a spiritual life. I struggled to keep up with the "dos," and found myself regularly slipping into the "don'ts." I couldn't live up to the ideals set forth by the church.

This made me feel as if I were disappointing everyone. Going to church started to make me feel bad about myself. I felt like they wanted me to be perfect, when in reality, I was a fraud, pretending to be someone I was not. I was constantly being reminded of my failure to measure up.

So I quit going. I have always been a perfectionist; I would rather not do something than do it poorly. This is not a good quality. It was, in part, the cause of my inferiority complex—and my guilt complex as well. I wanted to be perfect, but no man can live up to his own perfectionist ideals. No one is perfect; only God is perfect.

My primary reason for turning my back on church was that I didn't think I would ever measure up to the ideals and impossible expectations I *thought* others had for me. My life was marked by failure. I was plagued by guilt and shame. I read my inability to be "good" enough as an indication that I was "bad." Not only was I bad, I was bad in the eyes of God. This seemed like the ultimate failure.

This made me feel so desperate and terrible about myself that I dug in defiantly. I decided that, if goodness was beyond me, I would indulge in being bad. I wasn't supposed to drink or smoke? Well, then I'd have a pack of Marlboros and your cheapest whisky. I didn't just quit church; I plowed down a road of rebellion. The legalistic church had failed me. I very much believed that this meant that God had failed me, so I turned my back on Him.

The Importance of Discipleship

I had that one experience with God as a sophomore in high school, feeling Him fill my spirit in the church, before rejecting Him for many years. I ran from Him as fast as possible, barreling in the opposite direction—the wrong direction.

This was a difficult life for me. It was so difficult that I drank for years to be able to go through life without God.

Despite turning my back on the church, I never shook that first personal experience with God. He had touched me deeply that day. I knew in my heart that the experience was real; He had spoken to me directly. He had put out His hand and laid it upon me. This was one of the many defining moments of my life, and I was forever changed that day. I simply didn't know what to do with the experience at the time. I didn't know what to do with myself.

The choice to distance myself from God was my own. While I am wary of blaming the church for my own bad behavior and foolish mistakes, there is a way in which the church failed me: it failed to offer me true discipleship. I had undergone a powerful experience that could have resulted in transformation, but no one walked with me through the experience. I had seen a great truth without realizing its full weight.

God had touched me, but I did not know Him; I didn't know His word. The Gospel is powerful and instructive, but without discipleship, I had no one to help me interpret it. Walking with God is a journey few men can go alone with any depth of relationship. I needed someone to help me make that journey. I needed spiritual guidance and someone to help me make sense of my experience and recognize it for what it was.

If the church had offered discipleship, I might have taken a very different path in life and saved myself and my family a lot of misery. Instead, I turned to alcohol to numb myself. I would not get the discipleship I needed until much later, when I found it in Alcoholics Anonymous. Twelve-step programs are not just about overcoming addiction. They are about overcoming spiritual brokenness. They require you to surrender yourself to a higher power and find purpose and meaning in life.

I had already quit drinking when I joined Alcoholics Anonymous, but alcohol still had control over me. I thought about drinking all the time. As a "dry drunk," I was managing to stay sober, but the same destructive thinking that had caused me to drink continued to wreak havoc in other areas of my life. I maintained an inferiority complex and remained stuck in a cycle of guilt and shame. I hated myself. I was sober, yes, but I was still miserable. Without a doubt, I needed help to *stay* sober.

I never really expected to find salvation in Alcoholics Anonymous. I wasn't ready to commit to sobriety over the long term. The only reason I had shown up was a fear of my own depression and suicidal thoughts. But I didn't want to go even as I walked into my first AA meeting, skeptical. I was volatile, angry, and entirely unreceptive.

Thankfully, there was a man at my first AA meeting who took the time to listen anyway. He deflected my anger and pushed past my defenses. After the meeting, he pulled me aside to talk. We went outside and discussed why I'd come. He invited me over to his house so that we could chat further. I agreed, and off we went.

He was about ten years older than me, but further down the road of recovery. He told me about himself, but he mostly wanted to hear about my problems. He gave me a chance to open up and blow off some steam. He allowed me to share where I was in my own thinking.

This was the beginning of what would become a very important relationship. He agreed to become my sponsor. Twelve-step programs famously employ a sponsorship system in which veteran members sponsor and mentor newcomers. This is crucial for people who are just getting sober. A sponsor offers moral support in times of weakness. My sponsor went above and beyond this call of duty. He not only helped me stay sober, he also helped me find and walk with God. He gave me what I should have gotten in church as a boy: *discipleship*.

My sponsor helped me confront and address not only my addiction to alcohol, but also my spiritual brokenness. Alcoholism was merely the symptom. He helped me come to understand my underlying spiritual disease. He was the first person to sit me down and talk me through my relationship with God. In addition to carrying around the *Big Book of Alcoholics Anonymous*, he also had the Bible. I thought this was strange at first. I wasn't fully ready to come back to God yet, but God is exactly what I needed. My sponsor helped me to see this truth.

This was *not* a mentor-mentee relationship; we connected on a deep level that I hadn't known was possible between friends. He was my guide at first, as I started down the road to sobriety, but we were walking the path together. It was a symbiotic relationship. We both supported and challenged each other and held each other accountable.

My sponsor functioned as what I now consider a "work disciple." The operative word here is *work*. This kind of relationship was neither easy nor quick; the process took years. We started meeting almost every day after work. Sometimes we went to Alcoholics Anonymous meetings, as well as leads, where men would meet and share stories about their struggles and lives. Other times, we just met at home. We would spend three or four hours talking through my problems, my problematic thinking, and my spiritual brokenness. He guided me on my personal journey to find what I wanted in life, which was a better relationship with God. He taught me how to practice forgiveness and acceptance. He worked with me to achieve humility.

This was an intense and intimate process. It was confessional. I had to bare the darkest and ugliest parts of my soul to another person. I told him about my drinking and drug use, as well as the bad things I had done while intoxicated. I described my emotional abuse of my wife. These were hard things to say to another person, and tough to admit to someone else—much less myself. But doing so was the only way to work out my problems and let go of my self-hatred. My sponsor taught me about forgiveness and how to forgive *myself*.

Addiction is a downward spiral of doom and gloom. You use chemicals because you feel bad, and in turn, using makes you feel even worse. It is a cycle that brings people to the darkest parts of their lives. My sponsor armed me with the tools I needed to step out of the darkness and helped me bring my darkest moments to light. This was painful and hard, but it allowed me to escape the cycle of guilt and shame that sent me back to drinking.

The more I spoke, the more I was healed. Talking instilled me with a sense of freedom. I came out of the shadows and saw the light and the beauty of life. Little by little, day by day, I got better. At some point, I looked back and realized I didn't even have the desire to drink. I no longer wanted to be numb. I wanted to feel and to live life.

The Healing Power of Community

For his discipleship, I owe my sponsor a debt of gratitude, one that can never be fully paid back—only *forward*. The work I do at the Refuge now is an extension of my attempt to do for others what my sponsor did for me. I want to build the same kind of work-disciple communities that saved me.

My sponsor was key to my recovery, but he was only one part of a larger community. I was also forming other relationships within the Alcoholics Anonymous network that were equally important to my healing. We walked through the hard times together and shared in the joy of sobriety and living true to one's self. When we weren't going to meetings or working the

Twelve Steps, we participated in recreational activities. I often went out for dinner and movies with my sponsor, which was very important. I was learning to have fun without drinking. He was teaching me how to be a regular sober person.

I was also forming relationships in church at that time, which was crucial to my introduction back into the wider community. I had begun attending church services regularly, as well as recreational events. I played basketball with fellow church members, and I was making real friends for the first time. Finally, after years of self-imposed isolation, I was again feeling connected to other people.

This was a very healing time for me. I was reentering the world and launching into a new season of my life. My attitude had improved and my depression was lifting. I was more positive, charitable, and generous to both myself and others. My relationship with my wife and family improved, and my suicidal thoughts disappeared. I still struggled sometimes, as I was still in the process of healing, but I was hopeful. The path was long and arduous, but it felt manageable. I actually *wanted* to live.

The changes in me were visible to others. Our pastor would ask my wife and me to help others in the church who were struggling. He asked us to share our testimony in front of the church on several occasions. This was healing for my marriage. My wife and I were working side-by-side helping others. Within about a year, I was practically a new person. I wasn't perfect but I was healing. I was walking the Twelve

Steps. I had admitted my powerlessness over my addiction and had surrendered to my Higher Power, which is Jesus Christ. I had taken a moral inventory and made amends to the people that I'd hurt, especially my wife. I was engaging in new relationships and healing old ones. I had discovered community.

Above all, I had finally found my way back to God. I spent the year learning to communicate with Him, which took me on a spiritual journey. I learned much about God, but I learned even more about myself. For the first time, I had real faith. I had always been drawn to the church and liked the idea of God, but I now gave myself over to Him. I did not question; I just believed. That is faith, and it was what I had been missing. I only found it by taking myself off my own pedestal and dedicating my life to something greater than myself.

Community taught me about the importance of service. I began to recognize the importance of service to *healing*. I had been given so much, and I now wanted to give back. I dedicated myself to Alcoholics Anonymous and made it a point to go out and help other alcoholics and addicts. The twelfth step calls upon people recovering from addictions who have undergone a spiritual awakening to reach out to other alcoholics and people with addictions. I did just that; I sought them out and talked to them.

Ultimately, a desire to be of service to others led me to start hosting my Promise Keepers group. As I mentioned before, Promise Keepers was a popular men's movement in the church. Participants would meet to discuss their personal lives and spiritual lives, as well as the areas where they intersected. The idea was for men to hold each other accountable while trying to walk God's path.

This is similar to what I was already doing in Alcoholics Anonymous. Promise Keepers allowed me to take the same model and bring it to the men in my church. Many of them had their own struggles with alcohol, depression, marital strife, and other issues. It was a direct extension of what I was already doing, as well as a way to integrate an accountability model into other areas of my life beyond Alcoholics Anonymous. I was now able to serve other struggling men in addition to those at AA meetings.

People began congregating regularly in my basement for Promise Keepers meetings. Men from the church came together to support one another. We were baring our souls and sharing our hearts and our struggles. I was finally able to take off my mask and be authentic. Not all churches do this sort of thing—but they should. This is what I needed. It is what many men need, whether they struggle with addiction or other problems. There was a sense of safety and confidentiality. Men could discuss anything that was bothering them. We talked about our lives, our marriages, and our families, as well as our relationships with God. We learned about ourselves together, and we grew together.

These men became some of my best friends. This was new to me. I had been a recluse prior to going back to church. I didn't have many real friends, much less good ones who were a positive force. Now I had people in my life who could help me walk the right path, which for me was God's path. We were walking the path together, being of service to one another, and holding one another accountable.

So much healing took place in that basement. Marriages improved. Divorces were avoided. Addictions were overcome. Toxic thinking was banished. I experienced all of this myself. My life was improving in every way. I was thirty years old and believed that I was born again through Jesus Christ. My wife and I were mending our relationship, and I was feeling less depressed, because I was letting go of insecurities. I was no longer trying to please others. I was taking off my mask and showing the true me—warts and all—so that I could improve myself. Sobriety was still a struggle for me, but I was hopeful and doing much better. I was back in my community, contributing to people's lives in many ways, and finding kinship with other men who wanted the same things that I wanted.

This is when I really started to grow and change as a person. Alcoholics Anonymous had helped me get sober, but for at least a year, I was still heavily broken. I wasn't drinking, but I *wanted* to drink. I wasn't happy and wanted to numb my pain. This only changed because I reconnected with the church, continued renewing my thinking through study and meditation through the Bible on my spiritual journey, and joined Promise Keepers. I wasn't just staying sober; I was looking at myself in new and different ways. I was exploring new ways of being a man in the world.

This was a big step. I had struggled with insecurity my whole life; I had never been able to look in the mirror and like what I saw. This began to change, and I started to see the good in myself, which was only possible once I accepted and owned up to all the bad in myself. I hadn't been treating people well or loving my neighbors. I hadn't been taking care of my wife and children properly. Never had I been responsible or productive. My own accountability was a foreign concept to me. Now, I was doing all those things—and my new communities were helping to hold me accountable. I was overcoming the cycle of guilt and shame that had kept me debilitated for so long.

Promise Keepers showed me the healing power of community. I realized how, working to serve each other, we can bring about our salvation in everyday ways. It is not only that we were helping to heal each other; the act of helping was actually healing us. Service and community are always healing.

I carried this knowledge forward with me in my next big endeavor—starting the Refuge. My desire to be of service to other men who were still broken led me to ultimately abandon the newfound safety of my newly sober life, sell everything, and move to the country to serve the Lord and people who are lost.

Brokenness: Coming Down to Your Knees

My personal story of addiction has been hugely influential upon my work with the Refuge. I know what the men who come to us go through and the struggles they face. They are not just struggling with addiction. They are broken and there is a void they are trying to fill with the wrong things. There is only one thing that can fill this void and truly satisfy the soul. Healing their lives is not simply a matter of getting them to stop using and drinking. This emptiness or void needs to be addressed. What is fueling this desire to numb out? What is the source of the pain? Is there another way to deal with life's problems and stresses? Of course, the answer is yes, but these are questions that must be explored. No longer can we avoid getting to the root of addiction. This is why the Refuge is different from many other addiction treatment centers. We believe God is the only thing that can fill this void and heal the root of pain fueling the addiction and desire to numb out. It was receiving the love of my heavenly Father that changed my life forever and healed my heart. It is what filled the void.

Discipleship requires a willingness to address these underlying issues and transform into better men. As a population, people with addictions are generally not inclined to change. Change is hard and painful. Those with addictions want to keep using chemicals and stay numb. Most only start to change once they are in so much pain that all the alcohol and drugs in the world can't drown out the pain. **Change typically only occurs once the pain of the status quo exceeds the pain of changing.**

Brokenness is terrible; it causes pain. And while pain, by its very nature, doesn't feel good, it can be a powerful motivator. It can be transformative. The whole purpose of pain, the reason it is unpleasant, is that we will start to avoid the things causing it. The pain of brokenness can drive a person struggling with addiction to change his ways; it is one of the few things that can bring a man to his knees and transform him. But this is only once a threshold of pain has been breached and the man is ready to change.

It can be a beautiful thing when pain leads a man to transform by surrendering himself to God, which allows him to reach his full potential. However, he must be *willing* to transform. He can't just wallow in the pain; he must use it as fuel. For most people, this happens once they surpass a level of pain tolerance. In the parlance of the Twelve Steps and discipleship, the addicted person must first hit rock bottom.

For most, hitting rock bottom is only a matter of time. The men who come to the Refuge are at the end of their ropes. Their lives have become unmanageable. They have been to some dark places—for many, prison. Quite a few have suffered trauma and abuse. They have done terrible things to other people and are reeling from the guilt and shame. Many have overdosed and nearly died. Some have faced extreme violence in the pursuit of chemicals. They have all kinds of ailments, from cirrhosis to blood-borne diseases. They know they are near the end of the road.

In my line of work, I have seen every type of brokenness imaginable. Many men come in looking like corpses. Their eyes are dead and their expressions are blank. They have tried everything else and it failed, leading them to utter desperation. They pull over at the Refuge because it is the last stop before going over the cliff.

This can be devastating to see, but it is also beautiful. Desperation is fertile soil for transformation. When people finally hit rock bottom, there is nowhere to go but up. That's when people finally stand up, dust themselves off, and start climbing back up toward a new life. Their current life is unbearable, so they crave a new one.

Then, and only then, do we accept them with open arms at the Refuge. At that point, we provide them with housing, employment, community, accountability to the Scripture, and the chance to be of service to one another. Many of the men stay on at the Refuge as volunteers and employees because they feel the same calling I did.

In retrospect, I now see that God was trying to give me this calling for a long time. I was working on my business one day when a line of Scripture burst into my head and heart. It was Luke 4:18:

The Spirit of the Lord is on me,
because he has anointed me
to proclaim good news to the poor.
He has sent me to proclaim freedom for the prisoners
and recovery of sight for the blind,
to set the oppressed free.

The last line really hit me hard— "to set the oppressed free." At the time, I didn't understand what it meant or why the verse had come to me at all. I was neither actively religious, nor was I going to church. It had been years since I had read the Bible. But the passage resonated with me deeply. That it came to me seemingly from nowhere felt important.

I did some research into what it meant. I called a good friend who was a pastor and talked about it with him. He provided context on the Scripture but couldn't provide insight into why it had come to me. It was only much later, after having my vision and being given my calling to start the Refuge, that this made sense. I now see it as God trying to give me my calling. He was showing me the importance of service to community and asking me to actively work to help those who were still broken and struggling. This Scripture, Luke 4:18, was stated by Jesus as he read from Isaiah 61. This would be my road map to stay on mission to serve God.

A Look Inside
the Refuge Process

CHAPTER 6

Who We Accept at the Refuge

We wish that we could accept every man who comes to the Refuge, but unfortunately, space and funding are limited. There are only so many beds and so many rooms, only so many donors and partnering businesses that provide opportunities for the men to work. All of this caps the size of the program. We have been growing over time and are always looking to expand even more.

The selection process is crucial to achieving maximum results. We don't want to waste resources on men who aren't ready yet. Having worked with thousands of men over the years and having seen our fair share of both successes and failures, we have become good at identifying men who are ready to make the attempt. We cannot determine who will actually succeed. Many men try and fail despite their best efforts, but we're able to identify many men who will *definitely* fail. These are individuals who aren't ready to even make the attempt.

We vet applicants using a set of three critical criteria. We want to find men who are

- willing to change,
- ready to make a personal investment in that change, and
- ready to participate in group support and be accountable.

Meeting all the criteria does not guarantee that a man will quit using, work on repairing his broken life, and begin his spiritual journey. The criteria simply identify individuals who are ready to *attempt* to make the transformation.

The Willingness to Change

The goal of the Refuge is metamorphosis. We want to help broken men transform into functional, spiritually fulfilled individuals. The spiritual component is essential to what we do. We are a Christ-centered organization, and we believe that men must know God to know peace. We want to help broken men develop a relationship with God so that they may find His word. God both heals and transforms lives; I have seen it hundreds of times.

Transformation has always been central to our model and mission. Romans 12:2 says, "Do not be conformed to this world, but be transformed by the renewing of your mind." That word *transformed* means "metamorphosis"—the same complete change a caterpillar must go through to become a butterfly.

When I walked down to the creek in Vinton County and asked God if I was making the right decision in buying the farm, He revealed Himself to me with a fluttering multitude of butterflies. At the time, I was unaware of Romans 12:2, but ever since I became aware of it I have seen symbolism in butterflies, as they are the result of radical transformation. Caterpillars spend their lives crawling around before building themselves a cocoon and undergoing metamorphosis. They emerge as butterflies that then soar into the sky. The butterfly represents freedom, and that is our goal—to set the captives free.

This is what happens at the Refuge. The men come in having crawled through life. Some are *literally* unable to walk. They come to us and undergo a metamorphosis. There is a story of the butterfly that my wife found. The story goes like this: There was a boy walking along and he found a cocoon on the ground. He saw the butterfly struggling to get out of the cocoon. He decided to help it by making the tiny slit in the cocoon bigger. As the butterfly emerged he noticed that the wings did not look strong but rather weak. The butterfly was unable to fly as the wings would not work. The butterfly's body was very big and full of fluid. The boy then realized that because he made the slit bigger, the butterfly did not have to push through the cocoon. Therefore, the fluid could not be pushed from the body to the wings of the butterfly. There is a purpose in the struggle and the pushing. After the struggle and pushing, the fluid is pushed to the wings and the butterfly can fly wherever it wants. The same is true for these men. There is a purpose in the struggle. Though the butterfly may want to give up and quit pushing through, it doesn't quit. The result of not giving up and pushing forward is freedom and beauty. We forget that freedom is not easy to obtain and does require commitment and endurance. If all goes well, these men leave ready to launch into life and soar. They leave transformed, which is our goal. We even call one of our buildings in Vinton County the "Transformation Center."

To have any hope at discipleship, people struggling with addictions must have a strong desire to change. They must want to stop using. This must be a pure, raw desire to change for change's sake. They must be doing it for themselves and as a result of their own free will, as no one can force transformation upon them. The decision to change is the addicted person's and his alone. If he is only quitting for his wife, he is liable to start using again when she is not around. We have had parents who dragged in their children with addictions by the scruff of their necks. This never ends well. The person may *begin* to change, but he will fall off the wagon if he is not doing it for himself. If the person for whom he was attempting to quit lets him down or leaves in disgust, then the person with addictions has lost his motivator. He reverts to what he wants to do. He must want to change regardless of what anyone else wants or thinks.

We at the Refuge cannot force anyone to stop using, either. We cannot force someone to walk a new path. All we can do is offer him an opportunity; he must be ready and willing to take the first step. The journey has to be each man's own undertaking. We can only guide by our own example.

This doesn't mean people cannot influence a person with addictions. No one should act as an enabler. Spouses, parents, friends, and everyone else in the person's life should exercise tough love to exert influence. The addicted man cannot quit using for his wife, but he may quit using because *he* wants to keep his wife. He just cannot be doing it for *her sake* alone; he must want to change for his *own* benefit.

This is why pain is so important. Brokenness leads to addiction and causes pain. Most people struggling with addictions have very painful lives, so they continue using to numb the pain. They don't change, because change is hard, and they can keep using to stay numb. It is only when the status quo becomes more painful than change that a person becomes willing to change.

Once this happens, the transformation can begin. People with addictions may have moments of clarity in which they are able to see their problems clearly, and perhaps even understand that they are their own problem. Upon conceding this point, many people are ready to surrender to Jesus. This is the first step of any twelve-step program, and it is indicative of a true willingness to change.

Making a Personal Investment in Change

Surrendering to change is difficult for people with addictions. Even *more* difficult is investing effort in the change. One can surrender to change in a moment, or at least claim to do so, and then take it all back in the next breath. Therefore, we at the Refuge look for men who are willing to make an investment in change, because that requires actual sustained effort.

The people who succeed at the Refuge don't just *want* to change; they are *committed* to change. They are sick and tired of being sick and tired. They want a new life and are willing to act to make that a reality. People cannot simply "surrender" and then wait for God to fix their lives for them. They must get started in tangible ways and actually do the work themselves.

This is where things get really tough; walking the Twelve Steps is not easy. Reaching out to people for forgiveness and making amends takes both humility and strength. Remaining sober, humbled, and positive is hard; one has to stay the course. Twelve-step programs encourage people to take recovery one day at a time. This is so that they don't become overwhelmed. Making *sustained* change is difficult, as it is a huge commitment. No one becomes addicted overnight, so no one should expect to transform overnight.

That's OK; newcomers don't need to fix themselves in one day, or one week, or even one year. But they do have to be willing to get started. You can't move a parked car; you have to put it in drive and give it some gas. You have to get into motion or you'll never get anywhere.

The best way for a man to get started is to open his heart to healing and truth. Ask tough questions. When did I begin this crazy addiction journey and what were the circumstances or events that may have fed it? Was there abuse? Neglect? Was I introduced to drugs by my own parents? Was this generational? Was I trying to fit in? Begin to look inward and identify triggers. We encourage newcomers to first read particular books and watch videos about discipleship, as well as spiritual texts. The book that ultimately saved me was the Bible; I could not have begun my transformation without it. It was—and still is—my guidebook and serves as the blueprint for my new life. Study and exploration are great ways to begin making an effort and indicate a seriousness about and commitment to the process, but they do take work.

The Power of Group Support and Accountability

The Refuge is built around community and peer support. Our men attend group meetings and hold each other accountable throughout the day. This is an integral part of our model, and we require the men who come to us to participate in the community. The men need each other for support because maintaining sustained effort is very difficult. They also need each other for accountability. Any person attempting a big change needs others to hold him accountable. This is especially true of those with addictions. Their former lives were based on cheating and lying to get their chemicals, and habits like those are hard to break. Having accountability isn't just helpful; it's necessary. It's easy to slip up and backslide. In moments of weakness, we all need people to apply pressure and hold us accountable.

Group support creates fellowship and community at the Refuge and is extremely important to the process. People with addictions need peer support from people going through the same problems. Positive role models can provide success stories that newcomers can look to for encouragement and inspiration. Observing others going through transformation provides proof that one can do it too; simply seeing change is proof that change is possible. It gives hope to broken people who have gone for so long without it.

Offering accountability is important to recovery and healing as well; it builds character. When the men see one of their brothers slipping, they offer a hand, as well as words of encouragement. They help the individual stay the course. This cannot be taken for granted. Broken men are often isolated and do not know how to reach out. At the Refuge, they learn to do so, and once they leave, they take those abilities with them back into the wider community.

The men at the Refuge must be willing to engage in two-way accountability. We rely on a give-and-take system in which all residents participate. People with addictions need fellow brothers to be strong and charitable when they are feeling weak. This kind of generosity and openness is foreign to and difficult for many people—but it is teachable. We can show people how to receive from others, as well as how to be charitable and offer support. We can offer discipleship on the process while helping those with addictions to walk a new path. We can teach them to open up and share with others.

It's a Spiritual Journey, Not a Spiritual Grind

These criteria are not meant to weed out men who aren't worthy of discipleship. We want all men to find themselves, to find God, and to heal and transform. The criteria are designed only to help us focus resources on the men who are most ready for transformation. This is how we make sure every dollar produces maximum results. We are constantly refining these criteria and all other business processes to ensure that we are being as efficient and effective as possible. There are a lot of broken men in the world, and we want to help as many of them as we can.

The criteria underline the difficulty of true transformation, but this should not be discouraging. We won't lie; this journey is not easy, but it is rewarding. What the Refuge proves is that broken men can and *do* get better. They can recover and heal.

Some of these rewards are immediate upon surrendering. Surrendering means stepping away from depravity, turning one's back on brokenness, and taking a new path to Jesus Christ. People who finally surrender often report a sweet sense of peace. They have been fighting against the task of surrendering for a long time. They have done their best to go it alone and plow forward on a path of self-destruction. This is a hard life. Throwing in the towel and giving oneself over to something greater is a relief. One no longer should shoulder the burden alone; he can now walk with God. Ephesians 4:22–24 says it best: "you were taught, with regard to your former way of life, to put off your old self, which is being corrupted by its deceitful desires; to be made new in the attitude of your minds; and to put on the new self, created to be like God in true righteousness and holiness."

Often, I can see it as clearly as a lightbulb being turned on in a dark room. I can see it in their eyes. There is a look of relief on their face and the slope of their shoulders even changes. It is nearly palpable. It's also infectious. The men can see and feel it in each other as they heal, bond, form new communities, and create better lives. This is part of the reason why the Refuge has been so successful. We have created an environment where men can come, once they are ready, and help each other walk with Christ.

CHAPTER 7

The Refuge Recovery Model

The Refuge has a recovery model built around what we call "work discipleship." We are Christ-based and while we are focused on helping people overcome addiction, we also address the spiritual brokenness that drives the addiction. People with addictions may be able to get sober without fixing their brokenness, but they will be hard pressed to remain sober. They will return to using unless they have something greater than themselves to live for.

As a Christ-centered organization, we help those struggling with addictions develop a relationship with Jesus. Nothing but Christ can fill their emptiness. They aren't broken because they are addicted; they are addicted because they are broken. Once they develop a relationship with God, they won't *want* to be addicted. They may still want to use drugs and alcohol, but they will be better equipped to refrain from doing so because they won't have the same burning need to numb their pain, because that void has been filled.

We help people with addictions transform and develop a relationship with God by immersing them in a trusting, safe, and biblical environment. We recognize that this approach isn't for everyone. We're not trying to heal everyone—only those who are receptive to a biblical model based on the Gospel—and we don't shun or disparage other recovery models. We fill an important niche and leave it to other groups to fill theirs. Our niche is to help men change by offering discipleship and helping them to walk with God. We help them find community in each other and in church. We help men struggling with addiction find healing through faith and service.

We cannot help men who are not open to discipleship, nor can we help men who are uninterested in developing a relationship with Jesus. We have to turn such men away. They are welcome to come back later if they decide that they want to try discipleship. We simply cannot accept people who aren't interested in a spiritual relationship with God, because that is central to our ministry.

Our process isn't the only way for people to change, but it is one way—and it works. I know because it worked for me. Everything we do at the Refuge is centered on giving men the same kind of discipleship and support that was integral to my own transformation.

Discipleship, or "following Christ," is key to what we do at the Refuge. In essence, we are helping addicted men walk with God and live out the Gospel in their daily lives. This is not something most men can accomplish on their own. Most people, especially those with addictions, need help following a righteous path. We offer them a supportive space to live, work, and receive support while they develop a deeper relationship with God. They come here to practice living as men of God with the support of others.

Our facilities, curriculum, and model are designed to help those struggling with addiction by walking with them through their problems. We want to help them find strength and power in something greater than themselves. They need help with transforming into a better version of themselves by following Christ's example. It isn't enough to just put down the bottle or the needle; they have to learn to live sober, accept their flawed selves, and be God's children.

Induction into the Ministry

People who are interested in coming to the Refuge are asked to attend our weekly orientation in Columbus, Ohio. This is the gateway into the program. On average, we accept five to seven men into the Refuge during the orientation. We only have space for about twenty-five men on the farm at any given time. Turnover is high, and not everyone completes the process. This allows us to accept more men some weeks than others and keep the standards high.

We wish that we could help every individual who attends the orientation, but we only have so many beds. This requires us to winnow the applicant pool to the men who are most likely to benefit from the ministry. There are several qualifications we look for in an applicant.

The first requirement, of course, is that he wants to develop a relationship with Jesus. We make it clear from the start that the Refuge is a faith-based, Christ-centered transformation model. The men must be receptive to this or we refer them to another program better suited to their beliefs. We do this out of love. What *we* offer is discipleship. We are helping to heal them by teaching them to follow Christ, so we are not going to be of any help to a staunch atheist who isn't open to a biblical culture.

The second thing we look for in applicants is a willingness to transform their lives. They have to really want to change. We cannot force anyone to stop using or to accept discipleship. These actions must be performed willingly. Men must be ready to stop using and open to the idea of living by the Scripture.

Though the admission process is selective, orientation is open to all; we do not turn anyone away. While we cannot accept everyone into the ministry, we cherish the chance to tell all about our mission and process. We want to spread the word about the healing power of Christ, but not everyone is ready to accept that path. We tell all attendees about what we do in the hope that they will one day come back ready to transform and attempt to live a spiritual life dedicated to God.

During orientation, we talk about the Refuge, our discipleship process, the different opportunities we offer, and how we work. We explain who we are, what we do, and why the ministry is set up this way.

We then interview the men to determine which among them are best suited for the ministry. Typically, the men give us all the information we need. The men who aren't receptive to God will usually say so. Those who aren't ready to transform will admit to this fact. We make sure they are seeking a spiritual transformation and that they meet our criteria for willingness (see Chapter 6).

Finally, we want to make sure they understand that the program is practical and hands-on. We teach them to be sober, productive men of God by having them behave like sober, productive men of God. No drinking or smoking is tolerated. They will come to the Refuge not only to live, but also to work. They will study the Bible and apply the Scripture to their daily lives at the Refuge.

We then select the men to accept into the ministry and provide the others with information about alterative programs elsewhere.

Detox

Many of the people who come to the Refuge must first undergo withdrawal. Some of the men can do this at our facility. While we used to deal primarily with alcoholics, the opiate epidemic has changed that, and now most of our men are addicted to heroin or synthetic opioids. Fortunately, these men can detox at the Refuge. Heroin withdrawal is extremely uncomfortable, but it is not dangerous, and it includes vomiting, profuse sweating, and severe discomfort for a week. Withdrawal is miserable, but it won't kill them. We encourage them to detox at the Refuge because we can offer support and a safe place to stop using.

Alcoholics are a different story. Withdrawal from alcohol and certain drugs, such as benzodiazepines, can cause severe effects, including seizures, hallucinations, delirium, and even death. These men need to consult medical professionals about their detox *before* coming to the Refuge. Very heavy drinkers may have to go through inpatient detox first. Alcoholics without a severe physical dependence may simply be given medications to wean them off the alcohol. We may choose to admit some drinkers with a doctor's blessing, but we ourselves are not a medical model; we do not offer any medication and do not have medical professionals on staff. Safety comes first. They can always come to the Refuge after completing an inpatient detox.

The Refuge's Recovery Process

Once men are admitted into the ministry, they will move through a four-phase process if they stay until the end. Each phase has a different lodging, curriculum, and focus. Each phase is led by one of our directors, and the men receive support from that director, as well as each other, volunteer coordinators, and our other staff members.

These four phases are as follows:

- Phase 1: The Discovery Phase
- Phase 2: The Relational Phase
- Phase 3: The Application Phase
- Phase 4: The Launch Phase

Phase 1: The Discovery Phase

Men who are accepted into the program take up residence in the facilities on our farm in the hills of Vinton County, Ohio. The farm sits on more than a hundred rural acres. This is the original piece of land we purchased when we first opened the ministry. It is the foundation of the ministry.

The men spend an entire month on the farm. They stay on-site, and we take care of their every material need. We provide food and toiletries. We clothe them. We provide housing and sleeping arrangements. They have everything they need. We pay for all their residential needs for the entire time they stay with the ministry. During this phase, the men must merely focus on walking with God.

They begin their journey in the middle of nowhere for a reason. The farm is two hours outside of Columbus, Ohio, where many of our men reside, a distance far enough away that they can live free of the temptation and triggers that kept them using. This is a short reprieve, but it allows the men a safe space to discover themselves and explore their relationship with God. The natural beauty and remoteness of the farm allow the men to focus on God and feel His unconditional love and acceptance. The farm is devoid of all the normal temptations of home; their dealer is not around the corner and their drinking buddies aren't down at the local bar. The men are completely removed from their daily routines and no longer have to face the normal stressors of everyday life.

We are careful to keep the men isolated for the entire month to protect this reprieve. The men are not permitted any contact with the outside world, which means no leaving and no visitors. This frees them from having to deal with troubled marriages and other relationships. They don't have to worry about their responsibilities, housing, or any other obligations. They're free to focus on personal growth and growing with Christ. They are free of alcohol and drugs, and can finally think more clearly.

The Refuge is about so much more than just sobriety. It is different from a typical rehab. Men don't come just to get sober; they learn how to *live* sober. They receive the practical tools and knowledge necessary to live sober lives and serve God and others. We teach them how to be productive and how to serve. This is how we help ensure that they will *remain* sober.

The best way we know for addicted people to stay sober is for them to develop their own relationship with God. What we offer are the tools to do this. We show the men how to live life in line with the Gospel. The Refuge is a structured environment, complete with training and mentorship, that allows the men to practice living out the Gospel in their lives.

The men are given many daily opportunities to develop their minds, bodies, and spirits as they learn about Christ the Lord.

We do for the men that come to the Refuge what my AA sponsor did for me: we offer them a vision of discipleship. We walk with them through the realization of that vision. We help them take accountability for their past, present, and future. We show them a spiritual understanding of truth. We offer them community and positive relationships, which they may have never had. Ultimately, we teach them how to serve and pay it forward by doing the same for each other.

This is a very healing process. Our directors and staff walk with the men through their personal problems and help them look to the Scripture for answers. They receive counseling and support on a daily basis—an hourly basis, even. We are there with them from before sunup till after sundown. The men receive one-on-one mentoring with the directors, coordinators, and counselors. They spend time participating in small-group discussions, talking through their problems and biblical solutions, and learning how to support one another.

During their time at the Refuge, the men work with staff to develop a comprehensive plan for personal growth based on biblical principles. These plans are custom-tailored to their individual needs. We employ the Bible and Scripture truths to help them make sense of their lives and to develop a plan to transform and find redemption through the Scripture.

Much of their time in phase one is focused on support, healing, and study. Since we are a *working* ministry in every sense of the word, we want to give the men a space to try out abundant living. This includes hard work and a sense of self-purpose. We want to retrain them to be productive members of society. The thirty days in Vinton County afford the men space to get their feet wet and try out a new way of living that is both sober and spiritual. This is just enough time for them to decide if a life lived for God is something they want to commit to over the long term.

That's a decision most men cannot make when they are actively using. We have to first get them detoxed, sober, and clearheaded. No one can make logical, responsible decisions while under the influence. Chemicals and addiction distort one's thinking. Sober decisions require freedom from these chains. People cannot make important life decisions about their future when they are still using because the chemicals will call the shots. The men must first get sober before they can reflect on what brought them to this point and where they want to go next.

Once the men have detoxed, they are ready to experience a new way of living. This is not *just* about being sober; it is also about seeing the beauty in living a spiritual life. In addition to recovering from addiction, they are undergoing a spiritual awakening and transformation.

By the end of their time on the farm, the men have gotten a taste of what it is to have a spiritual life. They have received support and discipleship. Hopefully, they have started the healing process. They are thinking more clearly and can now decide if the ministry is right for them. Upon successful completion of the first phase, the men are given the option to participate in our program in Lancaster. At this point, some leave the Refuge and return to their lives, often with some success. But most of the men need more support and choose to continue with the ministry.

Phase 2: The Relational Phase

After thirty days on the farm in Vinton County, men who opt to stay at the Refuge are moved to our facilities in Lancaster, Ohio. This phase sits on 134 acres, which allows for the same peace and quiet as found in Vinton County. The men are able to continue focusing on reflection, transformation, and healing. While the men are again in a farm-like setting, Lancaster itself is less rural than Vinton County. It is a bedroom community of Columbus with a population of twenty thousand residents. It is not quite rural, not quite suburban, and certainly not urban.

The dualistic nature of this setting allows the men to begin a slow acclimation back into society. They are far enough away from their lives to continue group healing and counseling unimpeded, and they can spend their time in Lancaster studying the Bible and trying to live out the Scripture. However, they are now close enough to Columbus to commute to jobs and receive visitors at a structured family-day event.

We chose the Lancaster location precisely for these reasons. During this phase, we want to keep the men out of the city—where they could access bars and drug dealers—but keep them close enough for loved ones to visit. Many have partners and families in the city, and we want the men to start rebuilding these key relationships. The men are now allowed to write letters and talk on the phone, as well as have visitors once a month.

Repairing broken relationships and forging new healthy ones are what the men focus on in the Relational Phase. Our counselors and directors teach them how to relate to people in a healthy way. The men forge close bonds in their peer support groups and start learning to trust each other and be trustworthy. These skills will aid them greatly when they leave the Refuge. They are taught how to have healthy, supportive relationships with other people by practicing with each other. They learn and practice sacrifice, discipleship, brotherhood, conflict resolution, and peer support and evaluation.

The most important relationship they will work on at the Refuge, bar none, is their relationship with God. A healthy relationship with God will benefit every other relationship in their lives. This is achieved through the study of God's word, praise, worship, and service. We assist the men in navigating this relationship through one-on-one and group counseling that focuses on discipleship. We help each man understand that God created him uniquely and for a purpose. The men begin to reclaim their lives and personal stories, which can be used as a vehicle to serve the Lord.

When not working with the Scripture, the men are working with their hands, bodies, and minds. Since the

Refuge is a *working* ministry, beginning in Phase 2, we require the men to begin working jobs in the city. We set them up with partnered employers who have agreed to hire men from the ministry. These businesses know our mission, understand the population we work with, and are dedicated to giving the men a chance.

Working is not optional. We have a saying within the ministry: "Those who don't work, don't eat." If they don't work, they also don't sleep in our beds, take shelter beneath our roofs, or access any of our other resources. We don't charge the men anything to stay at the Refuge—not for their housing, food, necessities, treatment, or anything else. But we do require them to work jobs that help pay their way and support the other men coming up behind them in the ministry. Many of the men come through the door penniless, but that is no problem as we provide them with all their necessities.

Like everything we do at the Refuge, this is based on a biblical principle. Numerous verses of the Bible require man to take personal responsibility for himself, his family, and his community. God also requires man to care for His other children. We know from John 15:13 that there is no greater love than laying down your life for your friends. The men learn this firsthand by making friends at the Refuge and supporting each other in the ministry. The money they earn working jobs with our partner employers makes up 60 percent of the ministry's budget. They are taking responsibility for and caring for themselves and others.

The men start off working part time. They alternate between living in Lancaster and working in Columbus. We currently have capacity for forty men at a time in this phase. They are divided into two groups when they arrive in Lancaster; one group stays in Lancaster and continues discipleship and biblical study for a week while the other spends the week working in Columbus. At the end of each week, they swap places.

Switching between Columbus and Lancaster allows the men to reenter society more slowly. They are allowed to acclimate to the changes, which is important because many men with addictions slip back into their old attitudes and behavior when they return to their former environments.

I have seen this with my own eyes. In the early years of the Refuge, we kept the men on the farm full-time for longer and then eventually sent them straight home. The failure rate upon leaving was high. Being immersed in the woods too long bored the men; they became too removed from reality. The men behaved like monks on the farm only to return to using when they arrived back home. They didn't know how to behave properly in the real world. They only knew how to be good in the isolated environment of the farm, and they weren't equipped to handle the temptations of real life.

Now that we acclimate the men to the real world, their success rate is much higher. After a month on the farm in Vinton County, the men get to spend two months alternating between Lancaster and our community apartments in Columbus. They get their feet wet in Columbus a little more each week before coming back to Lancaster for support and counsel.

The week spent in Lancaster allows the men to continue with counseling, curriculum, and Bible study. They make phone calls home and reconnect with family members as they continue to work through their problems. They are able to shore up after the previous week's work and reflect on the progress they made during that period of time. They can examine their development, their feelings, and their relationships, and reflect upon where they are and where they're headed.

The men spend the following week in Columbus at their jobs, where, in addition to learning job skills, they can apply what they have learned to their work and personal lives. They still face temptation—the people at work may be using drugs and drinking—but they now have the tools and support to make the decision not to partake. This is an active process of learning and application. They get to test out what they are learning each week in a real-world situation.

That's the ultimate goal: to have the men apply biblical principles to their own lives. This isn't about just reading the Bible; it is also about *living* the Bible and better yet, believing it. You can quote a verse but still not believe it or live it.

We do not simply cut the men loose in Columbus every other week. The last thing newly sober men need is to have idle time in the city. They work weekdays and then retire to group apartments in our Columbus housing community at night. They have access to support and Bible study in the evenings and on weekends. They continue to receive supervision, support, and discipleship from our staff throughout every step of the journey.

This timeline allows for a metered reintroduction to the real world, including its stresses and temptations, while still offering lots of support, community, safety, and discipleship. We have had much better results with reintroducing the men to society and the working world in this manner.

The men benefit tremendously from working. It gives them a sense of purpose and integrity. The week they spend working in Columbus is just as important as the week spent in Lancaster. Many of these men haven't held down real jobs in years, if ever. They must learn to work if they are ever going to integrate back into society. They must learn to be productive and disciplined, and they only learn this by doing.

For many men with addictions, *doing* is a novel concept. They have spent their lives taking from others and just existing. They haven't done much giving or been productive. They aren't used to working, especially the younger men who have been hooked on opiates. This lack of work experience can be a real impediment to trying to reenter the real world. They don't know how to work, and they don't have the right temperament or dedication necessary to show up to work every day with a smile. Many of them are practically unemployable, with no experience or skills. Quite a few have criminal records, and the inability to find honest work is a major cause of recidivism.

The men at the Refuge have an advantage in this area, as they benefit substantially by working with our partnered employers. The men gain skills and experience while they develop discipline and a can-do work ethic. They build character and learn how to support themselves and their loved ones through honest work rather than by scamming and stealing. They leave the Refuge better equipped to find permanent work, and with a much better résumé to show future employers.

This work arrangement also benefits the Refuge as a ministry. We are only able to accept men into the Refuge without a fee because the men help pay their own way. Since we never charge or bill them anything for room, board, or services, we must run the ministry on money from donations and the money that comes in from the men's jobs as they are learning or improving their job skills.

The men reap satisfaction from paying their own way and helping the men entering the program after them. Their work directly supports their own process and expenses. The money the men bring in from our partnered businesses accounts for 60 percent of the Refuge's revenue. The rest is from donations, often from people who have already gone through the process, become successful in life, and then decided to give back to the ministry.

This system has sustained us for years now. The Refuge is a nonprofit that has required sacrifice from many of us. No one is getting rich off what we do. My wife and I supplement our income by owning several restaurant franchises. The Refuge is a definite privilege to serve and a labor of love—love for God. Like many of the men who have gone through the program, I actually invest my own money into the Refuge.

By the end of the relational phase, the men are further into their journey of transformation and have begun the healing process. They are discovering the rewards of sobriety. They have begun a gradual transition back into work and are grappling with responsibility, commitment, and dignity. Having reconnected with the outside world, they are rebuilding broken relationships and are learning to trust and rely on one another. They have begun developing an intimate relationship with God.

Phase 3: The Application Phase

After the process is completed in Lancaster, men who remain in the ministry transition into the Application Phase. These men spend the next three months living full-time in Columbus, Ohio. They continue to reside in our group apartments, but no longer spend every other week in Lancaster. They work about forty hours per week at their jobs in Columbus, periodically rotating between different employers.

The purpose of this phase is to apply what they have learned so far to their everyday lives. They have been doing this all along, but the focus is now predominately on application of all they have learned on the job site and with their families.

This is the point at which the men's days begin to more closely resemble "regular life." They are working full-time, and they have much more freedom to make choices about how they spend their time and money. They engage in activities of the local church too, because we want them to start building ties to the religious community.

They now have more contact with family. In addition to making phone calls and receiving visitors, they can go home every other weekend as part of their acclimatization to normal life. Those with nowhere to go are free to stay in their apartments, but we encourage the men to start reaching out to people outside of the Refuge.

The men now receive a small monthly stipend that they may save or spend at their discretion. We recommend that they invest the money in a savings account or into their own personal growth. At this point, they are now working enough to pay most of their way through the program while also subsidizing the men who are following in their footsteps. We ensure that the men understand this fact. We want them to recognize their own self-reliance and responsibility, as well as how far they have come in their reliance on Christ. This can be a powerful realization for them. They have already transformed themselves from people with addictions to productive members of society. They are slowly weaning themselves off the support we offer, and, in turn, are beginning to provide emotional and financial support to the men coming up behind them in the ministry.

Great responsibilities come with these greater freedoms. The men are still in the ministry and must abide by the rules of the Refuge. They are required to remain committed to following a biblical path in life, and they must support each other. It is necessary that they also begin actively planning for life after the Refuge. Volunteer coaches meet with the men weekly to provide discipleship and guidance, walking alongside the men as they begin this preparation.

While the men continue to receive support from staff and each other, the focus now shifts from one-on-one counseling to prayer and preparation. The goal was never *just* to get them sober; we want to get them onto God's path and ready for the future. If they slip off the path after leaving the Refuge, all their hard-fought gains were for naught.

We support the men through this planning process. They receive training in various skills, including child support issues, self-care, business acumen, and basic life skills (such as getting a driver's license, renting a place to live, writing a résumé, and getting a job, etc.). We help them consider options for when they eventually leave the Refuge. They begin receiving training in one of the Three Pathways that most men follow after they leave the ministry. (More information on the Three Pathways can be found in the next chapter.) This training serves them well, both at the Refuge and beyond.

Phase 4: The Launch Phase

The final phase of the discipleship process is the Launch Phase. The men now prepare to launch back into their lives in Christ. They continue applying biblical principles to their lives while getting ready to return to society.

Much more autonomy and trust are given to the men at this point so that they can fix their own lives. They can see family more often and leave the facilities to attend church so that they can build lasting relationships in the local community. In the final month, they are even allowed to leave their jobs during the day to arrange housing, transportation, and other needs as they prepare to launch.

With this greater autonomy comes even more responsibility. The price of freedom is accountability. The men continue to hold full-time jobs with our employment partners as they serve the community and the church. They begin to take on leadership roles in the ministry and set a good example for men just beginning the program. This prepares them to lead in their homes, churches, and communities as responsible men of God.

Refuge staff and volunteers continue to offer discipleship and support in this phase. Life mentors volunteer to teach the men the skills they need that will help them with all the important things in life—big and small—that need to be done. We help them apply for health insurance and get a driver's license if they still don't have one. They are offered assistance in figuring out transportation solutions. Many of the men have never accomplished these very basic things.

All these tasks are factored into their launch plan. Each man is assigned a personal mentor in Columbus who will help him devise a successful launch. This is his guide and advisor with whom he will consider short- and long-term goals, draft a budget, figure out where he will live and work, determine how he will get around, and decide how he will pay for expenses.

The three most important line items in the launch plan are transportation, employment, and housing, and we help the men plan for each of them. We will vouch for them to landlords and help house them directly. The Refuge is building its own housing community on the west side of Columbus. We have set up a rent-to-own program run by men who have been through the ministry. This allows the men to stay in a supportive community of like-minded individuals with whom they can form support groups, attend church, and enjoy life.

We place a strong emphasis on working in the ministry to help ensure the men find steady employment upon launch. The men leave the Refuge much more employable because we rotate them through different positions with our partner employers while they are in Columbus. This gives the men exposure to different working environments and roles, and by the end of their time at the Refuge, they have gained vital skills and experience in many areas. They have also forged personal connections with a variety of local businesses. We help them transform these connections into secure, permanent jobs when they complete the ministry. While there are no guarantees, many are offered full-time employment by our partner employers.

Other men go on to find employment outside of our network. We help the men put together a résumé and career portfolio that highlights all they have learned and accomplished.

By staging mock interviews, we teach them how to successfully communicate with potential employers.

In short, the final months at the Refuge are designed to help the men launch back into society as responsible, productive men of God. We help them devise a plan to go forward and succeed in life, just as they succeeded at the Refuge. We remain with them even after they leave, helping them to find work, housing, community, support, and—of course—God. One of the key factors is connecting to a local community church and serving in an area of their gifts. This is one of the most crucial things the men need for long-term success and accountability.

Willingness to Stay

The men must complete this process under their own volition. They are neither committed into the Refuge by someone else, nor are they there by court order. They are required to abide by our rules as long as they are at the Refuge, but they are free to leave anytime. We only accept the ready and willing.

We cannot force the men to stay and wouldn't even if we could. The voluntary nature of the process is a feature of the model. The ministry is not something men with addictions *have* to do. The process only works if this is something they *want* to do. They have to desire discipleship and a relationship with God, and they must be receptive to what we offer, or we cannot help them.

Most men do not make it through the entire process. About 40 percent of them drop out in the first month. Some aren't able to commit fully, some find the residential model too constricting, and some decide they don't want to participate in a Christ-centered program.

Some men come and get sober only to see themselves clearly for the first time, and they don't like what is reflected in the mirror. Many men who leave during the first month prefer to just stay numb, so they drop out of the ministry and go back to using. But those who are committed to the process work to allow Christ to transform them.

About 60 percent of men make it through the first month in Vinton County. Of those remaining men, about 70 percent stay for the whole two months in Lancaster. Most of the men who remain after this phase—approximately 80 percent—stay for the entire time in Columbus and then launch. All told, only one in three men makes it through the ministry from start to finish. We are focused on quality, not quantity, of disciples.

These numbers may sound bleak, but they are actually quite good in comparison to traditional recovery programs, which have much higher dropout rates. We consider this good news but don't take too much pride in it. The men who fail do so because they aren't ready to be sober and live a life for God. We hope they come back or find peace somewhere, somehow, but all we can do is offer what we have available and hope the men will accept it.

CHAPTER 8

After the Refuge:
The Three Pathways

Men currently spend about ten months in the ministry, working their way through our four-phase process. However, their journey does not end when they leave the ministry. We continue to offer them support even after they launch back into society as newly minted men of God. We connect each of them with a long-term mentor who checks in with him regularly and helps hold him accountable to his long-term goals for growth and development.

Our hope is that the men never *completely* leave the ministry. We believe discipleship is a lifelong process and we want them to remain a part of the Refuge's wider community as they move forward in their lives. The hope is that they will continue to serve each other and offer discipleship to other broken men for the rest of their lives. Those men who stay connected to the community definitely have a better chance at staying sober and being successful.

The men begin to consider what comes next before they ever leave the Refuge. Every man will have to chart his own individual path, but he will also have to continue to develop and tend to three different identities:

- his identity as a child of God,
- his identity as part of the local church, and
- his identity as a servant leader whenever God calls upon him.

These three identities are interrelated. For example, a man's identity as a child of God is directly related to his standing within the church and community. The men work on developing all three identities at the Refuge, but we pay extra attention to the third one. Service to God is what binds men together in the church and in their communities.

Service is healing. It promotes personal development and growth, and keeps men from returning to their old selfish, self-centered ways. Without the sense of purpose that service to God provides, many men serve only themselves. This is destructive enough for most people, but among men who struggle with addiction, this often leads to using. With nothing and no one else to live for, a sober addicted man will return to his drug of choice.

Whatever the men do once they leave the Refuge, it is key that service continues to play a major role in their lives. They need to venture out into the world and serve God and others.

They must pay forward that which they have been given. They came to the Refuge seeking discipleship, received that discipleship, and were healed by it, so now it is their turn to offer discipleship to others.

The Three Pathways

We created the "Three Pathways" to help the men continue to serve God after they finish their discipleship process. They are encouraged to choose one of the pathways while they are still in the ministry, and our staff will help them prepare for their chosen pathway during the Application and Launch phases. Each man will receive specialized training that will help him succeed in the path of his choice so that he will be prepared to become a servant leader before he ever leaves the Refuge.

Pathway 1: Refuge Coordinator

Men without committed relationships or responsibilities outside of the Columbus area can choose to apply to be a coordinator at the Refuge. This is a house-manager position with responsibilities that include coordinating the men's day-to-day activities, setting a healthy biblical culture at the ministry, and supporting the directors in serving the men in the ministry. We currently have space for about nine men to work at the ministry as coordinators, but we are expanding the opportunities all the time.

The selection process is intensive. The coordinators, who are our "boots on the ground" and the bedrock of the ministry, have a lot of responsibility at the Refuge. Without them, we would not be able to provide as much direct support to the men. We set high standards for the coordinators, as well as the rest of the staff.

Coordinators are provided with room and board plus a small stipend in return for which they must commit to staying at least six months. Their contract can be renewed only one time for another six months, after which they move on and give another man a turn. These are not long-term positions.

The time that men spend as coordinators is very valuable. Many men report experiencing more learning and personal growth as coordinators than they did while going through the ministry! Coordinator positions offer hands-on servant leadership experience, which is very valuable in that it can help launch future careers.

The ultimate goal for coordinators is to establish a permanent career elsewhere. We want the men to eventually reintegrate into the wider community. When their position ends, coordinators return to the community or pursue one of the other two pathways.

Occasionally, we are able to offer long-term employment at the Refuge, but these positions are few and far between. Typically, they are not filled by recent coordinators. We mostly hire men who went on to pursue higher education after leaving the Refuge. They come back later to serve after they've learned more advanced skills.

For example, the director who heads up the first and second phases of the ministry went through the ministry twelve years before returning. He pursued an undergraduate degree in ministry and then founded his own church. Afterward, he came back to serve on our staff. Our Phase 2 care administrator was the very first man to come to the Refuge. He earned a master's degree in counseling before returning to us.

We hire our own success stories in order to support them as they seek to serve the men coming up behind them. They know the process and its transformative power; they've lived it firsthand. Some of our directors went through the process and became success stories. We consider them proof that our men leave the Refuge ready to serve and raise up others. We know this to be true because many return to do so!

The staff who work for the Refuge are not opportunists, and they don't come back to work at the ministry solely to earn a living. Some of our directors are highly successful people, most of whom have advanced degrees. They could land lucrative jobs elsewhere, but they have come back to serve the men that they once were.

We are very humbled by this. Our ministry was built upon the faith and sacrifice of many people, including the men who use our services. The blood, sweat, and tears of the very men who went through the ministry made it what it is today. Our staff members—coordinators, volunteers, directors, and everyone else—are here because they want to serve the Lord.

Pathway 2: Champions Network

Not everyone who comes through the ministry can become a coordinator. Many men have responsibilities that preclude staying to work at the Refuge. Many have spouses, families, and careers outside of the Columbus area. They are not able to join the staff or volunteer their time. They have to launch back into their own lives in their own communities.

While they cannot stay at the Refuge, they still want to help support the ministry and its mission after they leave. They still want to serve, and help their still-addicted brothers find God, recover, and heal just as they did. We encourage these men to pay forward their assistance by helping those struggling with addiction in their own communities. We encourage them to be active in their local churches and start their own Champions groups.

We have developed a resource to assist with this endeavor: We ask men leaving the Refuge to commit to being a Refuge Champion through our Champions Network. Champions are men and women who have gone through their own transformation from addiction and are called to serve the churches in their local communities to form discipleship groups for the addicted. They build relationships within their home churches in order to offer support to those suffering from addiction.

The Champions Network is just that: a *network*. Champions are active in their communities and build strong connections with home churches where they can serve. They work closely with local ministers to identify people struggling with addiction and set up discipleship groups within their home churches to offer support for these persons.

Champions receive ongoing support and guidance. We provide online training courses through the Champions Online University and offer an hour of monthly coaching to get new Champions started. We also broadcast a monthly webinar in which Champions share best practices and encourage one another.

The greatest resource available to Refuge Champions is the Champions Network itself. Champions connect with each other in order to develop and adopt best practices for cohesive care. Would-be Champions can use the Network to find existing groups to shadow and study. They can also request to have an experienced Refuge Champion, or even Refuge staff, visit their new group so that they get started on the right foot.

Our Champions are making a difference every day. The tools are there. The will to serve is there. Refuge Champions are setting up new discipleship groups for people struggling with addictions in local communities across the country.

Pathway 3: Project 614

The third option is available to men who stay in the Columbus area and who are committed to contributing to the local community by leading Christ-centered lives. This opportunity is open to men straight out of the Refuge, as well as those who have served as coordinators and who are now looking to take the next step. Project 614, operated by the Refuge Ministries, provides the men of the Refuge with a path to homeownership while complementing the community strategy for rebuilding this area of the city.

Project 614 exists to create Gospel-centered communities that contribute to the well-being and revitalization of distressed neighborhoods in Columbus by developing and financing affordable, safe, and sustainable homes for redeemed men of God. In combination with the Refuge, it is moving men from homelessness and hopelessness to homeownership! We are helping disciples from the Refuge achieve the American Dream of homeownership so that they can remain stable members of society, and serve others and God.

The driving mechanism of Project 614 is a community-driven, rent-to-own program that is helping the men to achieve homeownership, which allows them to start building up their own communities. Each man enters the program as a renter, and each landlord is a fellow alumnus of the ministry. The renter helps renovate the space and eventually becomes a homeowner through a rent-to-own process. In return, that renter will later help the men following in his footsteps rent places until they can purchase their own.

Project 614 is not *just* a homeownership program. We are building a spiritual community on the west side of Columbus. This is an economically depressed and socially distressed area that our men are helping to turn around. They are leading the way as men of God and building a community where they can continue to walk through life together and serve God.

In order to participate in the program, men leaving the Refuge must commit to living together in a Gospel-centered community. They must show a commitment to living out biblical principles in their everyday lives, and they must remain active in community outreach and the local church.

Project 614 is a microcosm of our greater goal. It is what we want for all communities. Our vision is to see responsible men of God owning homes and leading successful lives throughout the country and the world. We want men to break free of the chains of addiction, walk with God, and, in the process, transform their lives, families, churches, neighborhoods, and communities. We want them to find hope and love. We want them to find God and allow His purpose to encompass their lives.

Project 614 has been a long time in the making. The program arose out of what we have long called the "25/25 Vision" at the Refuge. We have always wanted our men to remain in Columbus and revitalize the community to the glory of God. The vision was to see twenty-five men own twenty-five homes by the year 2025. This is an ambitious goal that we have held for seventeen years. Through much hard work and service, and by the grace and means of God, the 25/25 Vision is starting to become a reality. Project 614 is now building the staff, volunteers, institutions, resources, and expertise to make this happen. We want to see Project 614's 25/25 Vision both fulfilled and exceeded as we create Gospel-centered communities that contribute to the well-being and revitalization of distressed neighborhoods in Columbus by developing and financing affordable, safe, and sustainable homes.

Community and Discipleship: Men Charting Their Own Paths

Project 614 reflects the importance that the Refuge places on community. The men who come to the Refuge are immersed in community from the moment they arrive. We continue to help them build community when they reenter the real world because we understand that they won't get far without launching themselves into a community.

Project 614 is just one way our men are building community. They are also joining churches and starting community groups. They stay in touch and continue to offer support and accountability. They serve one another.

The whole point of the Three Pathways is to make living an act of selflessness. This is a new way of living for people with addictions. Their old lives were about feeding their addiction—their most basic wants. Once on God's path, their lives are no longer about what *they* want; their new lives are about serving God and their fellow man. In doing so, the man also serves himself.

Of course, there are more than three ways to serve God; there are more than three paths to follow. At the Refuge, we continue to develop new pathways all the time. Currently, we are setting up a national program that will help those fighting addiction form discipleship groups within their church. We will roll this out soon and then look for other ways for those who have recovered from addictions to continue to serve. We are expanding the rent-to-own housing program, and we opened a church on the west side of Columbus, where my son is a pastor, to continue building community among the men of the Refuge.

While all people need this kind of community, people who have recovered from addictions especially need community to stay sober. Many relapse because they have no reason to stay clean and sober. They leave rehab and have nothing and no one with whom to connect. They typically don't go to church, they have no community, and they often cut themselves off from the world. They may succeed at finding a job and other trappings of success, but without community and service, they really have nothing for which to live. Isolated and depressed, many eventually slip back into their old crowd and their old ways.

What they need to stay sober is a reason to live, and that reason is *service*. They need to find purpose in helping others and building community. They need to offer discipleship just as it has been given. The Three Pathways are simply codified methods for men who have received discipleship to pay it forward in their community. My Alcoholics Anonymous sponsor helped me by offering discipleship, and I paid it forward to the men at the Refuge. They, in turn, helped others.

The men at the Refuge learn to do this while there; they practice offering discipleship by supporting one another. They later carry that same mentality forward as they launch into life. This creates a chain of replicative healing. One man lays down his life for another; then that man does the same for the next. In this way, we all learn to walk with each other through our darkest hours, and to walk with God through replication. Discipleship is a cycle that never ends.

CHAPTER 9

In Their Words: Testimony of the Men of the Refuge

I could give no better testimony of the good we do at the Refuge than that of the men who have come through the ministry. Many have been kind enough to provide a brief testimony about the powerful effect the ministry had on them. They speak plainly and eloquently of their spiritual brokenness and how the Refuge helped them to reclaim their lives. All of them passed through the Refuge, and some have come back to serve.

Doug Shotsky

I was born one of six children and raised on an acre of land just outside of Grove City, a suburb of Columbus, Ohio. My parents were blue-collar factory workers who remained married until my father passed away.

The Lord blessed me with athletic capabilities and intelligence from an early age. I was good at most things I tried. I had mostly A's in school and was an above-average player in most sports.

I was introduced to pornography at a young age, around seven years old. Around a year later, I was molested by a teenage neighbor, and the abuse lasted several years. I became convinced that I had HIV and believed I was going to die. I was terror-stricken.

However, my mother sometimes took me to church as a child, planting the seeds of a life lived for God. The Lord was pursuing me from a young age.

I had two older brothers, both of whom were involved in drugs and alcohol as teenagers. I had started using drugs myself by eighth grade. My use escalated in high school. I dropped out of school for a while, was almost expelled after coming back, and then took five years to finish high school. After graduating, I spent three years bouncing from job to job, using harder drugs, and heading down a path of destruction. I was running from others. I was running from myself.

I was twenty years old when I went to the Refuge. I spent three months in the ministry before going back to the old path of destruction. I returned five months later and remained there for a year. I encountered the Lord Jesus Christ at the Refuge. I know beyond a shadow of a doubt that God is real and that the only way to have true peace in my life is to give myself to Him!

After leaving the Refuge, I went back to drugs for six months, but then the Body of Christ picked me up and began mentoring me as I walked this new life in Christ out in the "real world."

I found a man of God who mentored me closely for the next three years. This was crucial to my survival and development. I worked as a waiter for seven years because the Lord taught me to serve others and to simply learn to be faithful in the little things. I started and ran a small landscaping business for five years and started Bible college.

This was a good time in my life. I met my amazing wife, a woman of God that would never have considered me had I not been truly walking with Jesus. We had children together. I finished Bible college and pursued a master's degree in counseling. I could feel the Lord preparing me for a calling.

We raised our family in a nice, small town and integrated with the community. I spent three years as a professional counselor, mainly doing crisis counseling. I worked with many people who had attempted suicide or who had overdosed on drugs. The Lord promoted me while I was there. Life was good.

In 2013, the Refuge was planning to begin a church plant, and my wife and I wanted to be a part of this. After years of minimal contact with the ministry, I reconnected through the Refuge's church. About a year later, Tom approached me about the possibility of coming on staff at the Refuge. This was an absolute dream come true! Within about a year, my wife and I sold our house, moved, and came aboard the ministry.

I have learned so much about faith and leadership since I joined the staff at the Refuge! I have much more to learn. Many things have happened in the last few years of being back at the ministry. My wife's stepmother and my father both passed away. My wife left a stable career at The Ohio State University to be a stay-at-home mother. While some men who left the ministry passed away from overdoses, so many men have gone on to live successful lives. I cannot count the number of lives that have been, and continue to be, changed at the Refuge by the grace of God!

I am passionate about my family, my wife, my children, and the men of the Refuge. I can't wait to see what the Lord has planned for my future! The journey seems to have just begun. I do not know what the future holds, but I know the Lord is faithful and always will be!

Daniel Ogden

I am thirty years old and from Washington Court House, a small town in Ohio. I was raised in a Christian home by a supportive, loving family. I went to a private Christian school up through the ninth grade. In high school, I was heavily involved in church and played the drums for our praise team.

At the end of my senior year, I got into trouble with the law for underage alcohol consumption. This was a wake-up call. I straightened up and got back on the right path. I enrolled in Bible college and studied to become a pastor. Ready to start settling down, I began looking for someone to marry. I met a woman who I thought was "the one."

Unfortunately, she *wasn't* the one, and we went our separate ways. I was angry and bitter and blamed God for the breakup since I had served him my whole life. I thought he "owed" me this relationship. I felt cheated.

From that day forward, I started doing things *my* way. I decided to play college football even though I had never played the game in high school. I couldn't imagine what would go wrong. My parents and I decided that I could attend another Bible college in North Dakota. It was a tiny nothing of a town in the middle of nowhere, but the football team was awesome. We won nine games and lost only one. I thought I was headed for the NFL.

That didn't happen. I spent only one semester there. After the season was over, I returned to Ohio. I got a summer job at a feed plant and started hanging out with college buddies from North Dakota.

I also started playing semipro football as a fullback. In our very first game, I tore my rotator cuff. The doctors put me on pain pills. I played two seasons of semipro football with a torn rotator cuff thanks to those pain pills. A year later, I had shoulder surgery, and my shoulder problem was fixed.

However, my addiction problem was just getting started. I was off the pills for two months when, one day, I was hanging a two-by-six and a nail broke. It ricocheted toward me and hit me in the eye, which was unbelievably painful. I had eye surgery and was put back on pain medication.

My addiction progressed quickly from there. I needed to look for more drugs as soon as my prescription ran out. I went from hydrocodone to oxycodone to heroin in the span of one year. I started lying, cheating, and scamming to get my next fix. No one could trust me. I hurt my own family.

Eventually, my parents were ready to kick me out on the street. This was my breaking point, but it was also my salvation. I turned to the Refuge for help and enrolled in its program for the entire thirteen months.

Over the course of a year, I learned so much. I discovered how selfish, immature, and prideful I had been. I found brotherly love and discovered that it takes other people to help hold you up. It was all very helpful. After my year in the ministry was up, I stayed on for the fourth phase and lived in a Refuge sobriety house.

During this process, God healed my family, relationships, and trust. Looking back, prayer is what saved me. God blessed me with a great job when I came out of the Refuge. I met a woman of God who held me accountable and helped keep me true. She held me up with prayer, and she is now my wife.

Shortly after we got married, she became pregnant with our first baby, and though this wasn't planned, we were excited for this new adventure. Unfortunately, when we went in for our first ultrasound, we learned that the baby had no heartbeat. My wife began to cry at the doctor's office. She doubted herself. However, calmness and peace washed over me.

"This is a God moment," I told her. "God is still good."

In time, we began to heal by turning to Jesus. We prayed for a miracle, and a miracle is what we got. We lost our baby, but we saw the event as a religious testimony. It was a tragedy. But it was also a miracle that God brought my wife and me closer together and closer to Him. Unlike in my younger days, I did not blame God; I dug into Him.

I would not be the man of God that I am today were it not for the Refuge, prayer, and God. Without all this support, the death of our child would have caused me to relapse. The death was a tragedy—but our faith, particularly *my* new faith, in the face of this tragedy, was a miracle. It was the Refuge ministries that gave me the tools to be a man of God. I thank God that my parents raised me right and that the Refuge ministry helped me realize that.

God truly honors His word. I am living proof.

Corey Sword

My life was utter chaos right from the beginning. My mother and father were both alcoholics and addicts. They used to argue and get into physical fights. I was molested by a male family member when I was only eight years old. My parents divorced when I was ten, and I went to live with my aunt and uncle.

By the age of fourteen, I had begun to mask my pain with alcohol and drugs, which led to addiction. My addiction just caused me more pain. I would use and abuse anything— alcohol, cocaine, crack, heroin, pills—whatever would get me out of my own head. I hated reality. I would drink, snort, shoot, or swallow anything that reduced my pain or consciousness.

By the age of twenty-seven, I had lost everything—a marriage, house, cars, jobs, and custody of my daughter. I had nothing left but my own denial and self-pity. My life was already over. I was at rock bottom and absolutely broken.

This is when someone told me about the Refuge and my life began to change.

I went to the Refuge in April of 2008 with the idea of getting clean from drugs and alcohol. What I gained was my sobriety, and so much more. Within thirty days, I had truly accepted Jesus into my heart. I was, through God's word and by Jesus's example, utterly transformed over the next year. The hand of Almighty God reached down, picked me up, dusted me off, and put me back together piece by piece.

With faith and obedience came restoration. God is the restorer of all things; it says so in His word. I know this because I am living proof. God not only restored me in my physical being, but also, more importantly, in my spiritual being. God gave me a marriage, a family, and a home that puts Jesus first. God restored my marriage and my relationship with my daughters.

I began to pay this forward. My wife and I could share the Gospel with my parents and lead them to the Lord before they passed away. I now lead a Champions group for the Refuge. It is a circle of men who meet to talk about difficult matters, hold one another accountable, and work toward becoming responsible men of God. This is what I learned at the Refuge.

I also learned that the Lord will give you the desires of your heart when you walk with Him. He has given me gifts and talents that I have used to start my own business to help build His kingdom. He delivered to me a vision of a window-cleaning business while I was still at the Refuge. I told people around town about it, and they thought I was crazy. But here I am, having made it through the Great Recession. It is now 2017, and I own a growing business called Transparency Enterprises. We have been in business for six years and are continuing to grow, thanks to God's provision. I have two full-time employees, one of whom is also an alumnus of the Refuge. My wife also started her own photography business, Transparency Photography.

God has blessed me with more than I could have ever dreamed possible, and I praise Him every day. I will always be grateful that the Lord used the Refuge to teach me about who He is and who I am. I learned how to be a godly husband, father, and son. I discovered a new intimacy with God, and I now build my life on a foundation rooted in Christ rather than in the self. I am no longer the man I thought I was; I am God's son, and it is by His amazing grace that I have been saved.

Mike Wells

I am from Columbus, Ohio. I had a good family growing up, but I dishonored them by choosing a lifestyle of drugs. I was always seeking acceptance by others and this always caused trouble. It was also the reason I started using drugs. First it was weed, then cocaine. I got mixed up in organized illegal activity to support my drug habit.

Eventually, I tried a few inpatient rehab centers. They didn't work. My cocaine addiction progressed, and I eventually started using heroin too. This was the beginning of the end. I ended up homeless, sleeping on the streets with a backpack for a pillow and a towel for a blanket.

I knew death was close. Thankfully, God intervened.

By March 2005, I was totally broken and ready for a true change. I was lying on a cold, tiled bathroom floor of a church when God came down and saved me. Three days later, I entered the Refuge. This was surrender. I knew I couldn't keep doing things my way. I needed to live my life God's way.

At the Refuge, I learned to submit my life to God. I discovered who I am in Christ, how to build a relationship with Him and others, and how to apply the Scripture to my own life. I gained so much from all of this. God restored my relationship with family, and I learned how to be a responsible man of God. My life has been better ever since.

I decided to complete my GED after the Refuge. This was a huge accomplishment since I had never considered myself smart enough for a formal education. I earned my GED and then enrolled in college. In the eleven years since leaving the Refuge, I have earned an associate's degree, a bachelor's degree, and a diploma from a Christian ministry.

I also met a wonderful woman to whom I have been married for seven years. As she is an assistant pastor, we successfully established a church in conjunction with the Refuge. I am currently the director in the first phase of the Refuge, overseeing the men who come to the farm in Vinton County to get clean and find God.

The Refuge helped me to trade my drug-based lifestyle for a lifestyle based on Christ. I don't chase drugs anymore; I follow Christ. Now I am able to share with others what Jesus has done for my life and walk with them in transformation every day.

***

In the cover photo, a ripple effect is shown on the surface of the water, created as the result of a single drop. The same ripple will repeat again when another drop is added, and the process will continue to occur as long as new drops are added. This image is special to me because it accurately represents my life and work at the Refuge. With every drop of blood, sweat, and tears that fell, the outward ripple effect could be seen in the growing number of contributors, volunteers, and individual success stories. One of the more personal recipients of the ripple effect was my own father, a man who would benefit from something of such spiritual magnitude that neither of us was truly prepared.

Ken Thompson (Tom's father)

I will never forget when Tom first told me he was selling his company and starting the Refuge ministry. I was in total shock! Here is a young man who had an excellent company, was making more money than I ever did as a superintendent of the Pike County Schools, and he is leaving this to work with a group of drug addicts—unbelievable! My first reaction was, "Tom have you gone completely crazy?"

His very controlled and gentle response was, "Dad, the Lord has told me several times to do this and I simply must follow his command."

I will not get into the many thoughts and questions that rushed through my head at that time; they would take up half of this book. But the general idea was that here is a young man who had good intelligence, with a wonderful wife raising four little boys ages four to twelve, who was leaving the American dream to start up a ministry that he had absolutely no training for, no financing for, no place for them to live, and no food to eat—go figure!

Over the years, as I have watched the emotional development of this godsent ministry and the change in multitudes of men from age eighteen to eighty, from the end of the road to working productive citizens, it has also made a changed man out of me. On March 16, 2010, I turned my life over to Jesus Christ at the age of seventy-three and was proudly baptized a couple weeks later by two of my sons, Chuck and Tom. Although I was raised in a Christian home, I believe watching God's work with the men of Refuge was the prime factor in my becoming a God-fearing Christian.

Needless to say, I am most proud of the accomplishment made by Tom and his people through the guidance of our Lord Jesus Christ.

PART 3

Time to Write Your Story

CHAPTER 10

The Mission:
How Will You Serve and Why?

The purpose of this book is to encourage you to pray and seek God about what capacity you are to serve in. My prayer and desire is that you are excited and ready to take action by starting an organization of your own or by joining an existing one. Pushing fear and insecurities aside, I want you to get out into the world and honor God by being of service to others.

This raises an important question: *How* exactly will you serve?

I pray that some people will choose to begin organizations that are similar to the Refuge. It would excite me to see similar ministries popping up across the country, helping men and women overcome addiction and discipling them as they build or rebuild a relationship with Christ. However, you cannot simply emulate *my* calling; you have to discover *your* calling. There are many ways to serve and honor God.

What Is *Your* Calling?

Life coaches often try to help people find their own personal calling by asking their clients to imagine what they would do with their time if money were no object. How would you spend your time if you didn't have to work to pay bills? What are you so passionate about that you would do it for free?

This thought exercise doesn't just apply to fulfilling personal desires. It can also help you find your calling and decide how to serve. The only difference is that rather than thinking of what you want for yourself, you imagine how you would serve others.

You may find that these two things—your personal calling and your calling to serve—are one and the same. This is not uncommon. People who want to serve in a grand way typically spend their free time serving anyway. True servants of God live to serve. They spend their nights and weekends honoring the Lord and giving back to others.

This was the case for me once I conquered my drinking and depression. Even before starting the Refuge, I was helping men overcome addiction and find God. I had begun discipling men in my Promise Keepers group and continued to do so in other church settings. If anyone wanted help in dealing with addiction or walking with God, I was there.

This was personally fulfilling and something I felt compelled to do. Discipling men is my passion. The Refuge isn't really even about the drugs and alcohol. Those struggling with addiction are our target population because many need help and I happen to have personal insight into overcoming addiction; however, addiction is just one symptom of spiritual brokenness. My real passion has less to do with addiction and more to do with discipling individuals.

I have always taken this calling very seriously, which is how I knew the Refuge was not just some whim. Those meetings in my basement were small, informal, and intimate, but we showed up every single week—whether it was Thanksgiving Day or Super Bowl Sunday. The meetings meant everything to the men who attended. We had genuine and authentic discussions in which we would hold each other accountable. We walked with each other, formed community, underwent healing, and deepened our individual relationships with God. We became the best of friends. Thus, I began to discover my passion for discipling men and facilitating a healing atmosphere.

Back then, it was just a part-time thing, but when I quit my job, gave up my house and savings, and moved to Vinton County, it became my life. I was going to do full time what I had already been doing those evenings in the basement. The Refuge simply gave me the opportunity to have a bigger impact.

I cannot tell you what your passion is; only *you* can choose how you will serve. My greatest piece of advice is you must also get the support of your spouse and family. Otherwise it could cause big problems in a marriage. If my wife had not agreed to join me in founding this ministry it would have never happened. Before we make any big decisions, we pray, and if we both don't have peace we don't do it. When we started our businesses, it was the same thing. The Bible says when you are married you are one flesh so you must pray and seek God. If God does not give you both complete peace about starting a ministry, it would be a good idea not to move forward until that happens.

Don't Mistake a Burden with a Calling

All organizations need a mission or cause. Nonprofits and ministries like the Refuge exist to address some burden in the world, and their mission is to relieve whatever this burden is.

Nonprofits are plentiful because there is no shortage of burdens in the world. The world is rife with suffering that needs to be addressed. While this suffering comes in many forms, you cannot simply pick any old burden and make it your calling. For example, you can have a burden for the homeless but God has not called you to build a homeless shelter. Many people over the years have confused the two. A burden is a person who says I just can't stand to see people standing out in the cold with no food or shelter. I need to volunteer at the shelter and bring in food. The question is do you have a burden or a calling? I had a calling. A call to build a place for men with addictions. Not everyone is called to start a ministry from scratch. Some are called to come alongside these people.

You have a burden and you come alongside the called man or women. Often a calling is something you have overcome with God's help. It could be a nasty divorce, loss of a child or financial crisis.

If you have a burden and automatically think it is a calling to build a homeless shelter, you may find it difficult to stay the path when things start to get tough—and they *will* get tough. None of this is easy. Many people abandon their calling as soon as they hit the first bump in the road. Even more are lost to attrition as the long grind of keeping an organization afloat becomes their new daily reality. They run out of money or hit another kind of roadblock and don't know what to do, so they quit. They feel very little regret for doing so because they had mistaken the burden for a calling. Pray about which you have. This is so important. Even when you are called it gets so difficult that you do think of quitting.

It is easy to mistake any old burden for a personal calling. A burden should be addressed by *someone*—but not necessarily *you*. You may feel burdened by some cause, injustice, or societal need, and want to help without actually feeling *deeply compelled* to take action. People can easily mistake a simple burden for a true calling because they *do* care about the cause, but this does not make it a calling. You can be interested in a burden and may even feel emotional about the mission, but unless you feel totally compelled to heed the call and receive divine confirmation and spiritual markers for doing so, the burden is not a true calling.

Unfortunately, many people make this mistake. They identify a problem or burden in people's lives and devise a way to help and alleviate suffering. These are noble goals, but they do not make the burden a personal calling.

I have witnessed this on several occasions, and I continue to see it happen to people who want to join the Refuge. Many men who go through our ministry think they want to stay on and serve at the end of their stay with us. They were helped by us and now they want to help others. Unfortunately, many quit almost immediately. They aren't bad or weak; they simply don't have a passion for our cause. They can see how the Refuge helps men and alleviates suffering, so they want to help people in the way they have been helped, but our calling is not *their* calling. Eventually, more appropriate opportunities come along and they leave. I do not fault them at all. Quite a few of them go on to exciting careers and callings of their own. I *want* them to leave and find their true calling. I want them to serve in the way that makes the most sense for them.

Abandoning a cause is not a tragedy when the person is simply helping someone else's ministry, as that person doesn't have much skin in the game. The stakes get higher when you are establishing your own organization. A man once came up to me after a church club event and told me he'd also had a vision about starting a place like the Refuge. He'd never made that vision a reality because he hadn't been willing to make the sacrifices; it hadn't been his passion. He'd felt the burden but not the calling.

Look for Spiritual Confirmation

Confirmations and spiritual markers can help identify your mission and confirm that it is your true calling. For me, and many people, a true passion will have a spiritual driver. You should feel compelled to act upon your calling. You may not even personally *want* to take up the mission—but you nevertheless feel *compelled* to do so.

I would never have started an organization to help men with addictions on my own. This was not of my own volition; God gave me the calling. Starting the Refuge was never something I personally planned for or even wanted to pursue. Had I not received the calling, I would have continued in my business.

However, God's calling was so intense that it compelled me to act. I knew almost at once that this was something that I *had* to do. It wasn't a choice; the Refuge was my true calling. After my vision of the Refuge, I would dream about it at night and it gnawed at me throughout the day. God was calling me to do this thing, and there was no way I could ignore Him. I would have to one day stand before Him and answer for my action or inaction. I chose to heed His call.

However, I still had doubts, even as I started to take the first slow steps toward building the Refuge. While signing the contract on the farm, pen still in hand, I feared I was making a huge mistake. People were telling me I was crazy. In weak moments, I wondered if they were right.

What helped me overcome my doubts was spiritual confirmation. I had been receiving markers that were pushing me down the path I was on: the vision itself, someone's suggestion of Vinton County, my meeting with the realtor who went out of her way to sell me the perfect stretch of land in a county where large residential acreage is rarely for sale, the strange encounter with the butterflies when I asked God directly for advice, and many more. Things kept lining up that drove me toward Vinton County to buy this farm to fulfill this mission. I felt nudged down the path the entire way.

I continued to receive confirmations that helped me keep faith through the journey. One spiritual marker after another confirmed that this was my calling. I could almost feel the hand of God pulling me along. Whenever the path ahead seemed impossible, we would receive donations, volunteer support, and charitable offers and deals. We were always bailed out of every bad situation. Eventually, I could no longer write off these occurrences as mere "lucky breaks." After so much confirmation, I realized it would be folly *not* to believe that God wanted me on this path.

Begin looking for confirmations like these. If the calling truly is from God, He will provide spiritual markers along the way. Perhaps you will be offered an opportunity to get directly involved working in the cause you have been considering. Confirmation may come in the form of things simply lining up and presenting a path forward.

Confirmations are sometimes a big break, but they are often subtle, so you should look carefully for them. They can be as simple as relevant information about your cause from a stranger, or an uplifting and strangely pertinent news story at a serendipitous time. You might experience small reminders of your cause throughout the day that seem to be pushing you to act. Do not dismiss these subtle confirmations as mere coincidence or chance. God doesn't deal in coincidence; He deals in providence.

Spiritual markers can give you the strength you need to keep going. Many people are scared to act upon a calling, and just as many struggle to keep faith when things get difficult. Many people don't even want to heed their calling; they do so because they must. But the work is hard, no matter how much you love it.

Take comfort in spiritual markers. They are a sign that you are on the right path, and they can give you the strength and inspiration you need to keep going. Spiritual markers often occur when you feel the most tested. Every time I began to question my own sanity or wisdom in heading down a path that made no personal or financial sense, I would once again receive confirmation that kept me moving forward.

Get into Motion

Free of practical restraints, how would you serve? What do you have a burden for? Do you feel God calling you to something? Remember what I said about the difference between a burden and a calling. Not all of you will be called to build a ministry from scratch. Some of you will. Some of you will feel led to partner and help those who are called. This is an important thing to pray about. Next, you need to go out and pursue that burden or calling *in spite* of any practical restraints.

This is when fear often sets in, but don't worry; that's a natural reaction. Your calling may take you by surprise. Perhaps it is something much larger than you had anticipated. Big undertakings require courage and what can be a terrifying leap of faith, but anything worth doing takes effort.

You will never achieve anything without actually taking action. Making your calling a reality requires you to stop dreaming and start doing. There's nothing wrong with fantasizing; that is how visions are born. But you eventually must move from fantasy to strategy, and then transition from strategy to action. Develop actionable steps and execute them. The journey doesn't start until you actually leave home.

You don't need your final destination in mind to get started. You just need a vision of what you want to create, a loose plan with first steps, and then start working toward that vision. Your vision might change over time, which is fine. There's nothing wrong with changing direction midcourse.

Adjusting course is inevitable. No matter how well you plan, you will make missteps, miscalculations, and mistakes. You will realize that something in your plan isn't feasible or produces the wrong results. Perhaps you'll decide that your final destination wasn't quite right and you need to switch direction entirely. No worries. Dust yourself off and try something different.

Setbacks, obstacles, and false starts are part of the journey. Embrace the lessons learned and remain flexible. Keep your end goal in sight, but don't get too attached to your initial conceptions. My mission has always been to disciple men, but I have continually refined the Refuge. We have changed and added programs, tweaked our processes and methods, and expanded the mission over the years.

This was all done on the fly. I could not have planned everything flawlessly ahead of time. Sure, write a five-year plan, but be ready to adjust it as the months and years go by. You cannot possibly know where you will eventually end up. Fortunately, you don't have to. You just need to know whom you want to serve and how, and then you must plan a *few steps* to move in that direction (not the whole journey). I could never have conceived of the Refuge's current form when we first started. I just had a few steps in mind: buy a farm, build some infrastructure, find men to disciple, and help them find God and live sober lives. The rest of the details shook out over time.

Overplanning can keep you from ever getting started. But you should not delay in taking the first step, because you have to keep things moving while you have momentum. You can't steer a parked car; you have to put it in drive and get on the road. You won't know if you're on track until you are in motion.

Develop a Plan to Get Started

You need a series of actionable steps, but the exact nature of those steps will depend on your goals, available resources, obstacles, competencies, and other factors. Although I cannot write out your plan for you in this book, here are a few general things that will help most people get started.

Step 1: Tell somebody about your vision. This is the easiest way to start getting your vision out of your head and into the real world. Talk to mature, like-minded people who are good listeners and who will act as a sounding board for your ideas. Explain what you are doing. Talk with them about your plans and begin getting their input.

Don't take any criticism to heart. This isn't about them and their opinions. You can take their viewpoints into account, but that's not the point of this step. The goal here is to get your ideas out of your head and into the world. You need to voice your ideas so that you can start thinking them through.

Only seek out people whom you trust to be positive. Avoid what I call "dream killers"—the negative people who disparage your ideas. Find people who believe in you and surround yourself with them. Get their advice. Get people praying for you.

After my initial vision of the Refuge, I told several trusted people about my ideas. Those with whom I did share my ideas were very helpful. I talked to my wife, of course, and I also told a trusted friend from church, about the vision. I explained what I thought it meant and the implications it would have on my life.

Sharing the vision was a big leap of faith; it made me very vulnerable. My friend could have dismissed me, but he didn't. Instead, he listened carefully without interrupting. When I told him I was serious about making the vision a reality, he told me not to worry.

"If the vision is really from God, it will come to pass," he said.

He didn't judge me; he just listened and let me air my ideas in the open. He was someone whom I trusted. He's the chairman of our board today.

Step 2: Put your ideas down on paper. This is not just to avoid forgetting the good ones; writing down your ideas also helps you work through your thoughts and arrange them into a series of steps. Putting your thoughts on paper helps you clarify them and allows you to turn them into a draft of a real, actionable plan.

Step 3: Start doing research. Investigate the field in which you want to serve. Get curious, talk to people, and visit places. Find out what there is to learn and who is already doing the work. Talk to the leaders of organizations that specialize in the same area. Doing so can provide eye-opening insights into what you can and should do. These individuals can be a great resource and can teach you about what is needed in the area so that you can look for ways to help.

When I was getting started, I visited a ministry in Illinois run by Pastor Bob Wheaton. Formerly a pimp on the South Side of Chicago, he had married one of his prostitutes, gotten saved, and started the ministry. Operating on a farm in McLeansboro, Illinois, the ministry sounded just like what I had seen in my vision.

I arranged a visit and spent three days living among the men with a friend who had driven out with me. On the farm, there were about fifteen men, most of whom were from Chicago. We slept in their facilities, took meals with them, and participated in their curriculum. We partook in their physical training, group therapy, and other programs. Afterward, I went to Chicago with the pastor to observe a program they were starting in the inner city.

I was very impressed with the entire operation. They were making it work on a shoestring budget. He was already doing the work so well that I questioned whether I should even start my own ministry. I considered getting a van to help recruit and transport men to his ministry. I even donated to support their work. This was money I could have put toward opening the Refuge.

I called my wife first to make sure it was OK.

"It's a really big chunk of money," I said, "but I really want to help."

"Tom, whatever it is, do it," she replied without even asking the amount.

I wrote a large check, which he tossed onto the desk without even a glance. I told him that I was considering simply supporting him instead of starting my own ministry.

"Let me tell you something," he responded. "What God's telling me to tell you is that you are going to be the one who needs to start this place. You are called to do it. Everything is ready for you. You're going to find no problem with the land. It's going to happen."

Then he prayed over me and sent me off.

I couldn't sleep for two nights, as my mind was buzzing. It was another spiritual confirmation that reassured me I was on the right path.

I gleaned a lot from that experience. I saw what was possible on a small budget. This wasn't the most "professional" ministry, but what he lacked in resources, he made up for in faith in God. I was inspired and excited to see what God could do.

This realization helped me make some tough decisions: Should I sell my business? Was buying a farm and starting my own ministry really the right direction for me? What would my ministry look like? Visiting someone who was already doing the work helped me make those decisions with confidence.

Within a year I was in Vinton County, buying the farm. That was how it all started: investigating my options and examining my true desires. Up until then, all I'd had was my vision and a vague sense of intuition. By researching my options, willingness, and personal capacity, I was able to put a plan into place and get into motion. Almost two decades later, we are still going strong. More than three thousand men have now experienced at least some portion of the ministry.

In summary, find your calling, discuss it with people, conduct research, investigate your options, define your mission, and look for people doing similar work in order to gain knowledge and inspiration. Finally, when the right door opens and opportunity presents itself, be ready to take the first step and get into motion.

The Spiritual Dimension of the Calling: The *Why* and the Why *behind* the Why

By now you have gathered that this book cannot tell you *what* your calling is or should be. Everyone has a different calling. God gives us all different tasks. Nor can this book tell you exactly *how* to achieve your calling. I can only give you general steps that will help you get started, but you have to come up with your own action plan. Only you can chart and navigate your journey.

What I can directly speak to is the *why* of your journey. Please note that I am working under the assumption that most people reading this book believe in God and have accepted Jesus Christ as their savior. There are lots of books on founding nonprofits and plenty of secular advice, but the fact that you chose to read a book by someone who founded a ministry suggests you are approaching this from a spiritual, probably Christian, perspective.

Assuming the above is true, you know that one day you will have to stand before God and account for your life. God gives each one of us a calling in life, and it is up to each of us to decide whether or not to heed that calling. Either way, we will one day have to stand before Him and answer for our actions. His ultimate judgment drives what we do in life and how we serve God.

This is *why* we serve in the first place. When you strip away everything else, the core of my motivation and my entire earthly existence is to honor God. My guiding light through all of this is my faith. Faith drove me to found the Refuge, and faith keeps me going every day; it has done so for almost twenty years now. My love for God and my need to perform service undergirds every decision made and every action taken.

God is why I get up every morning, and He is how I get through the day. I engage in service because I am a servant of God. It is as simple as that.

I certainly did not found the Refuge because I "wanted" to do so. This life is hard, and heeding God's call is rarely easy. We do not do these things because we want to do so, but because we are compelled to act. We do so, happily, because we understand that our callings are bigger than we are. Our callings aren't about us; they are about God.

The *why* of service is always to glorify God. I serve at the Refuge because God gave me this calling. I started the Refuge to honor His glory. This was His calling and one day I will have to answer to Him for it.

This philosophy is freeing. My faith allows me to not worry about what other people think. I don't have to be concerned about whether what I am doing is profitable. I don't even have to fret over whether it makes sense. None of that is the point.

My calling isn't even a decision to make; it is simply what I must do. God put the men of the Refuge into my care, so serving the men is serving God. That is why I do this; that is why I *must* do this.

Understanding why you serve has pragmatic applications. The *why* is my guiding light, informing how I run the Refuge on a day-to-day basis and keeping me focused on my calling. It stops me from getting off track, which is very easy to do when you are running an organization, especially as it grows.

Running a ministry—or any other organization—requires a lot of work. Being an executive forces you to focus on the minutia of day-to-day operations. This daily grind is pressing, and you can start to become so myopic that you lose sight of the overall mission. This happens all the time; people get into something to heed a calling and serve their fellow man, but they get distracted by the bureaucracy of running and growing the organization. They lose sight of the people whom they are serving.

The primary purpose of the Refuge is to serve the men, treat their addiction, heal their spiritual brokenness, help them determine their purpose, and produce opportunities for them to be responsible men of God. That is our mission, and it must drive everything we do. The Refuge does not exist to sustain itself. We are neither here to serve the staff nor here to serve my interests. We aren't even here to serve the ministry. We are here to serve those affected by addiction—period.

This is why I apply the same litmus test to every single business decision we make. I ask myself: Will this proposed action really serve the men themselves, or will it just serve the ministry? Will this move the men forward, or simply move the ministry forward?

These two concerns are linked—but they are not the same. What is good for the ministry *may* be good for the men, but not always. Any action taken must be designed to best serve the *men,* not the organization. This allows us to maintain integrity and keep the mission central to our operations. I would never allow the Refuge to devolve into a soulless institution whose main purpose is self-perpetuation.

I apply this litmus test to literally every single decision made at the Refuge, whether big or small. It drives how we operate and helps us stay focused on why we are doing this on a day-to-day basis.

For example, we apply the litmus test when deciding whether to partner with an employer to hire and train the men. The men will spend months working with these partnered employers, so that time should enrich their recovery. The men should be working in safe environments and in positions that will ultimately give them the training, skills, and leadership experience they need to move forward in life.

These are the criteria we use to select employers with whom we will partner. We don't want the men to be in an environment that will encourage temptation or backsliding. We want them to leave the Refuge with the skills to reenter society and lead a normal life. We want them to be safe.

We absolutely do *not* choose partnered employers based on how much money they offer. The money that the men earn working with our partnered employers pays for their room and board, treatment, and for the men who are coming up behind them in the program and are not yet working. This money is important to the Refuge as an institution. However, wages play almost no role in the selection process. We will turn down positions that offer the men higher pay if we don't think the work environment is right. We believe in quality over quantity because we are here to serve the men, not to blindly expand. I don't want to grow the organization unless it is fulfilling the mission to the best of its ability. The ministry is only here to serve those who need it.

Keep your eye on the goal and remember why you are doing this in the first place. It is very easy to lose sight of your original reasons once your organization begins to grow. Most people want to expand their organization over time. This is a noble aim and can allow you to serve more people. But options are rarely equal. You will have to decide between expanding to be able to serve more people or to better serve fewer people. Each decision must be weighed carefully. Of course, you will want to serve more people, but you do not want to sacrifice quality. Quality is ultimately more important than quantity. I would rather grow the Refuge slowly and better serve fewer men than grow it too quickly. I happily forgo money that could grow the ministry if it means better serving the men we already have here.

Keep your focus on the people you are serving, not the thing you are trying to build; otherwise, you will find you have built the wrong thing. Don't let process distract you from your motive. Process is important because it helps you get things done, but your motivation and decision-making should be based on the mission. And that mission should be based on serving God and

His children, not you or the organization. Apply the litmus test to make sure you are making decisions for the right reasons. You want to keep looking back to the *why* and making sure that you are staying true to the cause. You got into this for the calling, so stay in it for the calling.

Finally, don't lose sight of the *why* that drives you. God is what compels you to serve. You are doing all of this to honor His glory and exalt the name of Jesus above all names. One day you will have to stand before Him and explain the decisions and choices you have made. Be sure you are making them for the right reasons.

CHAPTER 11

Casting Your Vision: Effective Team Building and Leadership Practices

F inding your calling is not just a matter of deciding what you *want* to do; you also have to consider what you *can* do. Success at anything requires specific competencies. You must be knowledgeable about what you are doing or your organization will suffer. You cannot be incompetent and serve people well.

Don't let your passion lead to naïve undertakings. Passion will only get you so far. A passion for rockets won't get you a job at NASA unless you have been to engineering school. You might be passionate about aviation, but you won't be getting into the cockpit (I hope!) unless you are in the process of learning how to fly a plane. Similarly, you shouldn't try to start an organization without knowing something—or, preferably, *a lot*—about its services and mission.

I am a positive person with a "can do" spirit; many people are the same. But the simple truth is that sometimes we cannot do certain things. We need to know something about the field in which we want to work. We need to have the right knowledge and skill set. Trying to serve others in an arena in which we have no practical experience is likely to lead to failure. This is simply the truth; not everyone can do everything. We all have different skill sets, talents, and areas of expertise. Our brains and bodies are wired differently. Accept this and find a way to serve that matches your talents and areas of expertise.

This may or may not include starting a ministry and/ or working with people with addictions. This is what *I* do. I am always looking to help people start ministries, like the Refuge, that work with people with addictions, but that is only because I have expertise and knowledge to offer these people. I encourage others to pursue starting other types of ministries, nonprofits, and projects as well. Do what works for you and those whom you will serve.

You almost certainly have plenty to offer in the right areas, so don't despair. You just need to make sure that your calling realistically aligns with your skill set. If you are still trying to find your calling, stop and assess your own skills and talents. What do you already know how to do? People who are thinking of starting an organization probably already have a lot of work experience and many skills. For example, businesspeople generally have management and communication abilities.

I had no track record of running a place like the Refuge when we started—but I had a lot of pertinent experience. I had a business background, which is always relevant to running an organization. The ministry is not just a ministry; it is also a nonprofit organization. My business background helped with marketing, communications, bookkeeping, accounting, administration, and business technology. I had a job that put me in charge of all the finances of a local community college. I also taught business math at the community college. These positions gave me valuable experience. I knew something about how to buy real estate, build infrastructure, make deals, and set up an organization.

General business skills are great, but you probably also have some specialized skills. Are you a salesperson? Then you already know how to talk to and persuade people. Lawyers know the law and how to set up a company or nonprofit. People working in accounting or finance know how to balance books. Administrators know how to handle vendors and coordinate projects. Executives know how to make big decisions and run organizations. These may seem like basic skills, but they took years to acquire, and you can put them to use getting your organization off the ground.

Consider your specific industry background. If you work in medicine, you probably have very valuable experience that would be beneficial to many ministries or nonprofits in the public health arena. Social workers, after years of experience in helping people to access services, learn the nuances to offer such services most effectively.

However, you don't necessarily *have* to have work experience or formal training in the specific area in which you want to work. I have no medical background, and I had never worked professionally in addiction treatment before starting the Refuge. I did know a lot about addiction, though. I had been around people with addictions all my life. I was an alcoholic and I managed to get better by attending support groups and walking with God. The Refuge is merely an attempt to share what helped me. This personal connection to our mission made me not only passionate, it also gave me insight into treating addiction.

I also had a lot of experience in the work I did in my church and through Promise Keepers. I had founded and run support groups for men struggling with addiction in the church. On day one at the Refuge, I was prepared to work with people with addictions using a tried-and-true Christ-centered recovery model.

The bottom line is that you don't have to know *everything* about what you are doing, but if you want to improve your chances of success and be taken seriously, you should know *something* relevant.

Invest in Yourself

All is not lost if you don't have the competencies you need to pursue your calling. You can always go out and get them. This can be done directly by actually learning the skills you need.

Even if you do have some of the skills you need, it never hurts to hone them. Invest in yourself. Shoddiness and unprofessionalism aren't helpful to people. God expects us to invest in our talents to better serve others, so you should be engaged in a lifelong attempt to improve yourself so that you can be effective at doing so.

Consider education as an option for gaining the competencies you need. You can go back to school for a new degree or maybe just take continuing education courses. There are many nondegree programs that will train you in different skills.

I invested heavily in myself to improve the Refuge. I attended a school of ministry and received biblical training. I took biblical counseling classes, completed leadership-development programs, and studied public speaking. I received coaching and training. I invested thousands of dollars into developing myself so that I could serve the men of the Refuge—and I continue to do so today.

Find the Right People to Walk with You

This is a key point: You do not have to do everything yourself. You will not be competent in every area of your ministry or organization, so just bring something to the table and inspire others to join you.

Invest in yourself, and others will invest in you and your vision. They can help fill in some of the competency gaps. Surround yourself with people who are able to do whatever you cannot, but who also understand your mission. If you don't know how to do something that you are passionate about, find someone with the same passion who does. That person may be very willing to work with you as long as you also bring something to the table.

The people you let into your inner circle should have the same passion and commitment to the cause as you. Don't take in a computer programmer just because you need someone to build an enterprise system for your organization. Don't bring on a talented executive just because he or she has an impressive track record. Make sure all of your staff members truly believe in your cause. You aren't just staffing a business; you are staffing an organization that will help execute your life's calling. Your calling should be their calling too.

There is a good chance that many of the people you need are already within reach. Most people don't pick their calling out of thin air. They are already involved in doing the work before trying to start a ministry or an organization. Personally, I already knew many of the people who would be instrumental to the Refuge long before I opened the doors. We are a faith-based organization, and I knew many people of faith as a result of my involvement in the church.

While many good people are already within your circle, you should still be reaching out as much as possible. Expand your network. Share your vision with the world. Get it out of your head and in front of people so that interested parties can find you. **Cast your vision and bring new people to the cause.**

This is your number-one responsibility as the founder of an organization. You are the primary spokesperson for your vision, so you need to be able to articulate it and inspire others. Whether you are recruiting volunteers or trying to get a loan from the bank, you will have to effectively cast your vision and get people interested and excited. Casting a vision is how you attract people to the cause—how you find people with the competencies and passion that you need: staff members, donors, volunteers, and all manner of help.

Casting your vision requires you to be able to stand up in front of people and explain what you are doing and why. This is the art of authentic communication. Let people know what the vision means to you and why they should also care about the cause. Share your vision. Share your story. Share your *excitement*! You will know you have found the *right* people when they, too, are excited about your vision. However, you will not know that your vision excites them unless you can convey your message effectively; this is crucial to getting people on board.

Look for ways to amplify your voice so that you can cast your vision further and wider. Find platforms and soapboxes, real or virtual, from which to speak to a wider audience. Don't forget your *target* audience though. You want to reach more people who are interested in your cause, not simply more people in general.

Being active in Christian communities, I was already known to the local churches. When I was ready to start the

Refuge, they gave me a platform to get my vision out to a larger audience. Local churches invited me up to the pulpit to talk about the Refuge and share our story. I did this almost every weekend for the first three years. This was a great platform for sharing my vision to a large, targeted audience, and it worked. People would come up to me afterward and offer to help. They offered money, time, expertise, advice—whatever they had to give. I still engage in similar events regularly in order to get the word out, raise funds, and popularize our vision.

Modern technology makes it easier to cast our vision further and wider. Social media is a powerful tool for reaching new people and can be used for networking, publicity, and community engagement. Your organization should have a Facebook page that links to your website. Participate on Twitter and other platforms. You must be active online for this to work; you can't just throw up a page and then never log in again. Follow other people and organizations. Answer messages. Get involved in online discussions. Tell people what you do and invite them to events so that you can connect with them offline as well.

Building Your Team

Unless you are an organization of one, you will eventually need to assemble a team. This is a big task best approached in stages. You do not need to hire everyone all at once, and you don't need to make hires with an eye to five years from now. Most organizations start off on a shoestring budget and must use resources carefully. Focus on acquiring people with the competencies you need to start fulfilling your core mission, and wait until later to worry about later.

Many organizations that start out small, such as the Refuge, require founders to do much of the work themselves at the beginning. The Refuge started as my family and me. We brought in new people over time. Some of the first people you attract who come aboard may not be staff members. They may simply be mentors, but do not discredit the value of these people.

Over time, you will most likely need to build out a team. If you don't have the funds to hire people, consider looking for volunteers and partners. Grow the organization and gather resources. With God's provision, you will eventually be able to start hiring staff members.

This is eventually necessary for most growing organizations. You cannot run a growing organization on your own. You will need a leadership team and a well-rounded staff. You must acquire people who are good with money, people who are good with people, and people who are skilled at different ways of serving. It takes all types. The key factor and quality to look for is a servant-hearted person.

Nonprofits will need to form a legal board in order to attain nonprofit status. This means finding and selecting board members. Some people select board members solely based on the size of their influence, network, or bank account. They are selected based on "credentials." They may be an executive at an institution or a member of high society. This certainly has its benefits. Influential board members can help you network and locate bigger donors and opportunities. Prestigious board members can lend legitimacy to the organization.

However, this is not how I do things. I believe it is best to partner with people who share my passion for the cause. This includes partners, team members, volunteers, and board members. My board members were selected because they believe in the mission and are men of integrity in their own businesses and jobs. I know them personally, and we have a relationship. They are in it to serve the men who come to us seeking help.

Surround yourself with like-hearted people who will encourage and inspire you with their love of service. I don't want to work with people who are only in this for the money or status as a philanthropist. Most nonprofit board members do not receive much recognition, and when some people figure this out, they leave. The Refuge has been very fortunate to benefit from the service of persons not seeking attention.

This is particularly true as you grow and begin to offer paying positions. We have many volunteers who show up saying they want to serve, only to disappear after a few weeks. They come in and hang around for a while to see if we will hire them, and when we don't, they quietly disappear. These are not the people we want to hire, and they aren't the people we want as volunteers either. I understand that everyone needs a paycheck, but the Refuge is a small nonprofit. We aren't here to provide careers. We are here to provide for the cause. We are looking for people who believe in our mission first and foremost.

Look for pure-hearted people who don't want anything in return, as they are there to serve. Of course, there are many reasons that people want to serve, but the only truly *good* reason, from my perspective, is for the sake of service itself for the Lord. I want a team composed exclusively of people who *want* to serve. They shouldn't be doing it primarily for money or experience.

Also watch out for people who, while not motivated by financial compensation, are driven by some other personal emotional need. The Refuge once had an older couple volunteer. We needed their services and were happy for their help, but things quickly went south. The couple developed an unhealthy relationship with the men. They became entangled in the men's personal lives, babying and spoiling the men as if they were their children. The couple even started showing up on weekends to take the men on trips.

This was problematic. The couple was disrupting the men's curriculum and schedules. Their behavior was disrupting our process and endangering the men's recoveries. The couple's behavior had little to do with the men and everything to do with their own desires. They clearly wanted something out of this relationship that had nothing to do with helping the men. They may not have even been aware of this; however, their actions were about getting what *they* wanted rather than giving the men what they *needed*.

We asked the couple to stop volunteering because the whole thing was trouble—not just for the men but for the couple too! We work with men recovering from addictions, and people with addictions know how to manipulate people. Some of the men tried to manipulate the couple to get what they wanted. One man left the ministry, and we later learned the couple had taken him on a vacation! When they returned from the vacation, the man stole just about everything from their house. He took their prescriptions, guns, electronics, and anything else he could carry.

This is just one example of what can happen when your team members don't have their priorities straight. You need to find people who are coming in to be servants, not those looking to get their own needs met out of the process. They shouldn't have their own personal agenda. They can receive satisfaction from the process; I certainly do! But that satisfaction should be derived from serving. They should not put their personal agenda above the cause. We are always seeking people who are looking to serve the men and God, first and foremost.

The people we let serve at the Refuge, from the most part-time of volunteers all the way up to the board members, are there because they believe in the mission. The cause is as important to them as it is to me. They want to serve the men. They want to honor God through their service. They see the value in what we are doing and "get it." I don't have to worry about their commitment, as their relationship to the Refuge—and to me—is personal and spiritual.

When hiring people, I look for commitment to our cause, chemistry, and the competencies we need. People should be able to serve in the way we need them to and have a passion for doing so. They should believe in our mission and our methods, as well as have good chemistry with the Refuge and the people with whom they will be dealing. If they are serving the men directly, they should have good rapport with the men. If they will be handling donations, they should know how to relate to donors.

Find People You Can Trust; Then Trust Them

You must be able to trust your team. You *will* have to rely on them—both financially and emotionally. The people around you are there to support you.

Their support is more important than any grant could ever be. Money comes and goes. People come and go, too, but the best will be integral to your success. Some will stay for the long term. Even when they do move on, they will have left an indelible mark. The people who helped make the Refuge what it has become were indispensable. They have been our most valuable resource from the beginning.

One such person was a man by the name of Bob, who passed away a few years ago. Bob was crucial to what the Refuge has become. He was with me in the ministry for ten years. He started as a volunteer, came on staff, and eventually became the chairman of the board. He never accepted a single payment for any of it.

Bob was someone I could trust. I would have made numerous financial and executive missteps had it not been for his leadership. He walked with me every day. He was supportive and nurturing, and he took on major responsibilities. Twenty-five years my senior, he was a spiritual father figure and a *working* mentor. He never just gave advice; he showed up and taught me how to do things. He led by example.

Bob was a talented and knowledgeable man. Before retiring, he ran a construction business, so he helped us with construction. He helped with bank loans and the management of projects. He mentored the men. Sometimes he spearheaded projects, like the time he helped the men start an internal company that sold chicken through a mobile kitchen.

Bob would help with anything and everything. No task was too big; no task was too small. He wasn't afraid to pick up a shovel or file documents. He would even answer our ministry's phone. He was a true servant who believed in the mission.

"Just tell me what you want," he would say. "Anything you want, I'll take care of it."

Bob was driven by a desire to serve. He had been blessed in life. He had a wife and family, his own successful business, and everything he could ever want or need. God had given him so much. Now, he wanted to give back.

He told me this when we met at a golf outing that was a fundraiser for the Refuge. He told me he was getting ready to retire and wanted something to keep himself busy so he wouldn't drive his wife crazy. He didn't want to just roll out of bed and go golfing every day.

"I need to have something of value to do," he told me over lunch.

He wanted to serve—and he wanted to do it at the Refuge. Our work inspired him, and he yearned to be a part of it. He longed to give back to God through serving me. He gave to me so that I could give to the Refuge.

And, give back he did. Bob served for ten straight years, throughout his entire retirement. He was helping construct a building when he passed away from a heart attack at the age of seventy-six. The building was only two weeks away from completion. It was our last building, and he considered it his legacy.

Bob had come to the Refuge to give back, but within a year he confessed that the Refuge had become just one more blessing in his life. That made sense to me. Bob was a man who lived to serve.

You want to find people like Bob. He was dedicated to service and to our mission, and had competencies we sorely needed. He was a mentor to both the men at the Refuge and to me personally. He was doing it for all the right reasons.

Unfortunately, I cannot tell you exactly where to go and pick up a Bob. If I knew, I would go snatch one up myself. Bob was a gift from Heaven. His actual full name was Bob Holycross. I should probably have considered that a spiritual marker! He certainly acted as one. Bob gave me a sense of peace and made me feel like I was on the right track; he was confirmation personified.

What I can tell you is this: Keep your eye out for Bobs. They are everywhere. They are actually *looking for you*. You just need to cast your vision and get the word out, and they will find you.

Put yourself in places where these individuals will find you. Get involved with groups interested in your cause. Start volunteering yourself. Meet people. This is key to your success. Whatever your organization will do, forming relationships will be central to your job as a leader. Learn to build strong relationships, which is something you can only master through practice.

Visit other nonprofits doing something similar to what you want to do. When you meet people there, ask questions, shake hands, and go ahead and ask them where they found their people. You will learn new things and gain fresh perspectives. I visited several ministries serving people with addictions before starting the Refuge. None of these visits ultimately altered my basic vision, but each one taught me something. I met people who offered small nuggets of value or inspiration upon which I could build.

There is no secret formula for drawing the right people to your cause. You just have to do good work and get the word out. The rest you entrust to God.

It will get easier over time. Building out your network creates a snowball effect: The more people you know, the easier it is to meet more. People interested in your cause will know each other. Good people hang out with good people. Meet one good person, and he or she will introduce you to friends. Bob introduced me to many people who helped the Refuge. He would invite his buddies out to the Refuge for a visit, and they'd soon begin pitching in time and money as well.

Eventually, you will build a robust network that becomes self-sustaining. But it all starts with those first meet and greets, so put yourself out there so that the people you need can find you. Cast your vision powerfully.

Once you find partners, employees, and volunteers you trust, you must *actually* trust them. Trust is a two-way street; you will need to let your guard down and let people in. Bob came to me during an outreach event. He was open and honest. For my part, I simply threw the door open and let him into the inner circle. We built a real relationship on mutual trust.

I always strive to build relationships like these with people in my life. I am quick to trust people. Relationships make life more fulfilling. Strong relationships allow you to walk together with other people and hold each other accountable. I always want more great people in my life, especially if we are working together. This has paid off, both personally and at the Refuge. Without trusting people and letting them in, I would never have found someone like Bob.

Building trust requires both parties to open themselves up. You will need to support *each other*. Treat them well—as real people—and they will treat you well. Show them respect, and they will respect you. Be honest about the organization and what you do. Be transparent. Set clear expectations and standards. Communicate well. Tell them what is what—and if they want to stick around, let them.

I am not saying you should trust blindly or recklessly, nor am I saying that others will never let you down, or you won't let them down. In fact, I can guarantee you that sometimes you will be disappointed. Sometimes, people just can't be what you need. Trusting many people means that some of them will eventually disappoint you. That's part of the process and a cost of doing ministry.

What I *am* saying is that you will need people you can trust, and you cannot have people you can trust if you don't trust anyone. When you find individuals who seem trustworthy, go with your gut. It is better to give someone a shot and maybe get burned than to never have anyone around to help.

You *will* need help, so you will have to trust *someone*. As I mentioned earlier, I'm not saying you should trust blindly—but do trust.

Empower Your Team Members

Don't just trust your team members; empower them too. Give them ownership over the areas in which they serve. When I let Bob into my inner circle, I didn't simply trust him to do as I asked; I also trusted him to tell *me* what to do. I took his counsel, and I took it seriously.

Some leaders try to micromanage everything. Some won't even delegate; they believe they have to do it all themselves to ensure that it gets done to their standards. They let their insecurity, anxiety, stubbornness, or pompousness get the best of them. That's not a good way to lead.

Good leaders delegate and empower their team members to take ownership over their roles. You want your team members to feel able to hone their skills, improve, and grow. Allow them to grow with the organization, and provide them the opportunity to get better at what they are already good at.

Remember, you cannot run everything yourself or do everything yourself. Don't waste time doing tasks you aren't good at or interested in. Some people are just better at certain things. For example, my strength is executive planning. I focus on building, growing, and developing our ministry. I also like to work directly with the executive staff. I am not as good at some other aspects of the business. I am not skilled at schmoozing. I am straightforward and honest—good qualities—but no one has ever called me diplomatic. This is a good disposition to have when discipling people. It is less ideal when it comes to public relations or negotiations.

When people want to work with you, figure out what they are good at, and determine what interests them. Don't just assume; ask them. Let it be an interactive process. Enable them to use their skills to serve. Don't just delegate; empower them so that they can have an input and shape their roles and the organization. Don't stand in the way of good people; trust them to use their skills and talents effectively.

Allow them to expand their competencies so that they can better contribute to the organization, and be sure to get their feedback. Ask them how they are interested in serving and, assuming they are compatible with your cause, fit them into the organization in the best way possible.

Then get out of their way. I let my leadership team take ownership over their respective areas. They are doing critical tasks, but I have faith in the idea that they know better than me about what they have been working on. I trust them to tend to their own purview.

Our directors don't just deliver curriculum; they help develop it themselves. I let my marketing person control the marketing. I was terrible at marketing, while she is gifted. She can clearly and powerfully articulate who we are and what we do. She has developed our branding and helped us deliver our message to the right people. She has created our logos, she runs our websites, and she is in charge of the Refuge's public image.

Of course, I take an active role in everything we do. I retain veto power. It is ultimately up to me to keep the Refuge in line with the original vision. But I work with my team as part of a team. Our directors develop curriculum and our financial officer handles our budgets and assets, but we go over everything together as a team. We make big executive decisions together. I respect their expertise and consider their input carefully. I trust them unless they give me a reason not to do so.

Putting people in the right places allows them to hone their talents into real skills, and it will allow you to develop a fierce and well-rounded team over time. At the Refuge, we now have good communicators. We have people who are skilled in direct service. We have excellent planners and educators. We have a person who handles the books, P&Ls, and balance sheets.

The result has been amazing and far better than anything I could have realized through central planning. This is only possible because we have the right people in the right places, and we allow them enough autonomy to figure out what needs to be done. We empower every person at the Refuge to answer his or her calling so that, together, we can answer *our* calling.

CHAPTER 12

When the Door Opens, Walk through It: Managing Fear and Doubt

Spiritual confirmations of your path often come in the form of an open door: an important person offers to partner with you; a once-in-a-lifetime funding opportunity presents itself; or perhaps a learning opportunity is made available. Such doors as these may open unexpectedly and present a path forward for you to pursue your calling.

Open doors rarely stay open for long. You must be ready to seize the moment and rush through that door before it slams shut.

This is easier said than done. Big opportunities come with big risks. You don't always know what is on the other side of the door. It takes a big leap of faith to cross over the threshold. You are likely to have reservations about acting rashly. Doubt often creeps in and fear takes over. You stand there paralyzed until the door is blown shut. This happens all the time. Fear can lead to indecision and missed opportunities.

Fear and doubt are natural responses. They can prevent us from making mistakes. Unfortunately, they can also make us miss once-in-a-lifetime opportunities. Sometimes, you just have to act—and fast.

I am not condoning rash decisions. You need to think big decisions through. However, you can't sit on the sidelines forever. Eventually, you are going to have to step out on a limb and take a leap of faith, or simply abandon your aspirations. Otherwise, you will never get anywhere.

Things are less scary when you are just *thinking* about taking action. When I first received the vision, I was excited about the Refuge. Yes, I experienced fear and doubt almost immediately, but I was also excited. I would daydream about the possibilities. I liked talking over ideas with friends and confidants. Lying in bed at night, I had huge worries, but I was mostly enthusiastic.

I loved talking about the Refuge, and that's because talk is cheap. Everything changed once I was in Vinton County and had to sign on the dotted line for the farm. Suddenly, I was making a down payment and committing to the mortgage. It was the first tangible step toward making my vision a reality. This was no longer just talk; it was real action.

This was far scarier than just thinking and talking about the Refuge. Conversations and daydreams aren't legally binding.

Legal contracts *are*. This was my first major action toward starting the Refuge. It felt like a point of no return. Signing the papers meant I was really doing this.

The gravity of the situation hit me hard. It was no longer fun; it was *scary*. Was I really going to just throw my whole life away? Was I ready to sell my business and write off years of education and professional experience? Was I willing to jeopardize my livelihood and the security and comfort of my family? Was I prepared to yank my kids out of good private schools, separate them from their friends, and drag them out to an impoverished area in rural Appalachia? Was I willing to do that to myself and leave behind my church and community?

I had grave reservations. I had doubts—and not just about signing the mortgage, but also about the entire endeavor. Talk had been fun. This was not. The risks and sacrifices were suddenly very real.

I was overcome with fear and doubt. I was concerned about failure. I feared making a mistake; I even worried that the whole endeavor was a mistake. People had told me I was crazy, and I wondered if they were right after all. Maybe this was no vision from God and I was just nuts! I had to excuse myself from the realtor and the seller in order to think over the decision in private.

Fear and doubt can be paralyzing. They can cause you to stall before you ever begin. Had it not been for a small sign from God that followed, I might have backed out of the whole venture then and there. I am thankful for this confirmation and the boost of faith it gave me to carry through with my plan; otherwise, the Refuge might never have come to be. The reason it exists today is not because I overcame fear or doubt. The Refuge exists because I acted *despite* my fears and doubt.

Fear is a survival mechanism. There is nothing more human than fear. It is a sign of practicality and pragmatism. Those who feel no fear are not courageous; they are either foolish, ignorant, or naïve. Taking risks, going out on a limb, *should* result in fear. But while fear is natural, it is not always rational. Even when fear *is* justified, it does not necessarily mean you are making the wrong decision. In fact, it may indicate that you truly believe the opportunity you are about to act upon is the one you should take. The realization that your life is about to change can induce fear. Your adrenaline response can be a sign that you already know that you should act.

Whether your fear is justified or not, the important thing is not to let your fear prevent you from acting. There are many Scriptures about fear. John 14:1 says, "Let not your heart be troubled: believe in God, believe in me." Wow, my heart was troubled and I realized my problem was I did not believe God. So, this is where prayer comes in and not just reading but believing God's word. Also, Psalm 56:3 says, "When I am afraid, I put my trust in you." And my favorite verse is Matthew 6:34, which says, "Therefore do not worry about tomorrow, for tomorrow will worry about itself. Each day has enough trouble of its own."

While you are definitely going to struggle with negative emotions, you don't have to let them control you. You are going to feel fear; this is a natural part of living a life of faith. Acknowledge the fear but do not let it stop you from serving and honoring God. When a door opens, assess your options carefully. Do not let worry cloud your judgment or prevent you from making rational judgments. Don't let anxiety block your path; instead, walk directly *through* it.

Throughout the time I have been working at the Refuge, I have never fully extinguished my fear and doubts. I probably never will. You have to learn that fear is something you may feel, but it doesn't have to paralyze you. You can work through it. Courageous leaders experience fear, but they don't let it hold them back or stop them from what they are doing. Instead, they look to God and believe in Him and His promises. They don't conquer fear; they push through it.

Fear itself cannot harm you. Your reaction to it is what can paralyze you. If you can still act in the face of dread, then it loses its destructive powers. What matters is not that you have fear but how you react to it. As Franklin D. Roosevelt famously said, "The only thing we have to fear is fear itself." God Himself states "Fear not" hundreds of times in the Scripture I live by.

Let Your Faith Be Your Guide

The $64,000 question is: How do great leaders manage their negative emotions and move confidently in the face of fear and doubt?

There are many ways to manage these twin emotions. I can only tell you what drives me forward: my faith in God.

This is ultimately a question of motivation. You need to find something that motivates you so much that fear is no deterrent. What drives you? If you're like me, you are driven by an unwavering belief in God.

This is my foundation—and it is solid. I believe without question that there is a God and that I am called upon to serve Him. My particular calling was to build the Refuge and disciple men with addictions so that they may know the love and healing of God.

Belief in God is a powerful motivator. It keeps me going in spite of any fears or doubts. It gets me through my darkest times.

I recently lost a man at the Refuge. We found him dead in his room. He was someone who had gone through the ministry and gotten clean. He had been with us for quite some time, but then he relapsed and died. This shook me to the core. I felt discouraged, with familiar doubts about the mission. I wondered if we were really making any difference. I questioned my life and our entire mission. I questioned the very cause we were fighting for.

But, I didn't quit. I finished out the day despite how I was feeling. I showed up the next day and the day after. I kept moving forward. I kept showing up.

I would not be able to do this without my faith in God, for that is what keeps negative emotions and anxiety from paralyzing me. I believe in God and something bigger than myself. I know that, come what may, God will be there with me.

This doesn't mean I don't have bad days or that I don't get upset, feeling down, or scared. I am all of these much of the time. It simply means that I can carry on in the face of fear and doubt.

I was once deeply troubled by my doubts and fears. Doubt seemed like a literal failure of faith. I no longer feel this way. I have come to realize that doubt is not so much a failure of faith as it is a *test of faith*. There can be no faith without fear and doubt. Doubt is driven by fear, and fear is a response to hardship, obstacles, and the unknown.

These things are precisely why we need faith. We need faith most when we face adversity. This is when we remind each other to keep the faith, as if it were at risk of collapse. However, this is somewhat true; adversity does test our faith. But these moments of adversity are why we need faith in the first place.

We turn to faith when the road becomes difficult. We trust in God to see us through the hard times. If the path were easy and certain, what use would we have for faith? Why would we need to trust in God? What would "having faith" even mean?

This realization has changed my perspective on doubt. I no longer see it as a failure of my faith, but as a *driver* of faith. Doubt and fear remind me why I need God.

You are going to face adversity when pursuing your calling. You will have moments of weakness, but do not allow these times to throw your faith or calling into question. When the road is hard, you will have doubts. You may question everything you are doing and start talking yourself into quitting. If you start to feel this way, immediately *stop*.

Stop viewing doubt as a failure of faith. Obstacles and setbacks should not have you questioning your choices, your faith, and God. This is when you need faith and God the most.

Doubt *is* a test of faith. My advice to you is to not fail the test. Don't let fear feed your doubt. Do not let doubt deter you from your calling. Doubt and fear are not necessarily signs of misplaced faith. Fear or doubt about your calling does not mean it is false. You can—and will—have doubts and fears about a legitimate and true calling. The answer is not to turn and run. The answer is not to lose faith. The answer is to *double down* on faith. Work harder and trust in God.

The Long Road Ahead

Managing your emotions is not a one-and-done endeavor. The fear and doubt never completely go away. Fear has plagued me for years now. At times, the path ahead has seemed impossibly difficult. There have been countless times when I've awakened at night, wondering how to keep the lights on and feed the men the next day. I feared letting them down and making a fool of myself. I feared failing.

These kinds of fears never completely disappear; none of your emotions will. An undertaking of this magnitude will send you on a permanent emotional rollercoaster. Some days you'll feel sad and on others, you'll feel mad. On good days, you will feel happy, grateful, and accomplished. On great days, the fruits of your service will leave you awed. However, you'll only get there by pushing through the bad times. You must get out of bed, go to work, and continue onward. You have to work through the fear.

The task has not gotten easier over time. On balance, experience has not made the journey any less difficult on a day-to-day basis. *Some* things will get easier with time. You gain experience. You learn the field. You build confidence in yourself and in the organization through Christ. Overcoming obstacles builds confidence. You get to know God and trust Him. Your faith grows.

However, other things will become harder. The best-case scenario is that the organization keeps growing to serve more and more people. Hitting your goals leads to setting more ambitious goals. This creates ever-larger obstacles and difficulties: you are serving more people; you have more staff, and you are handling more money.

Things have not gotten any easier over the last twenty years, but the Refuge has gone from serving a single man to a hundred at a time. We have more resources, but we also have more responsibility. More men at the Refuge means more problems and complications.

Success can even cause new problems. At first, people in Vinton County were generally enthusiastic and supportive of our mission. Addiction affects not just the people with addictions, but also entire communities. Parts of Appalachia have been decimated by opioid addiction, so locals were initially happy for our help.

However, some people grew suspicious as they saw us growing and becoming successful. They maligned our efforts and accused us of exploiting the men's work, even though we don't profit from the Refuge at all. The men's wages go right back into the ministry's needs. The local paper ran a smear story. People would come up to us in public and hurl accusations. In Lancaster, we ran into problems with people who were fighting our efforts to open a new facility because, while they wanted people with addictions to get treatment, they didn't want that treatment to take place in their own backyard.

All of this exacted a huge emotional toll on my wife and me. But we didn't let it stop us from pursuing our calling. We went to public meetings. We did outreach. We tried to explain what we did and our positive impact. We shared our financials with the public.

Above all, we kept fighting and moving forward. We pushed on and opened the Lancaster facility and expanded our ministry. We kept doing the Lord's work.

And we are still doing that work today. It has never been easy. It never *will* be easy. But my faith allows me to carry on regardless. I really have no other option.

I know that I will someday be called to stand before God and answer for my actions. When that day comes, I want to be able to explain to Him why I answered His calling. I do not want to have to stand before Him and make excuses for why I failed to do so. This is a powerful motivator, in good times and bad.

CHAPTER 13

On Sacrifice: What Are You Willing to Give Up for Your Calling?

G reat things are not achieved without sacrifice. The larger the undertaking, the greater the sacrifice will be. You will have to invest time and money into getting your organization off the ground. Keeping it afloat and growing is a lifelong endeavor. Repeatedly, you will find yourself up against a wall and having to sacrifice even more to keep things going.

The costs are not just business costs; you cannot simply throw money at them. Money helps, but you will also have to invest time, sweat, and tears. The costs will be very personal because the calling itself is so personal. You will have to make changes to your life and give up things that you enjoy. You may have to move or sacrifice your career. Personal goals may be sidelined. You will incur rising opportunity costs as the years tick by. You may derail your education and career for years, decades, or even forever.

I gave up my house and my business, left my hometown, and moved away from my church and friends. I sacrificed financial security and the satisfaction of a career. I forfeited anything and everything to heed the call.

Since then, I have rebuilt much of my life. I have a new church, new local friends, and a new ministry. My wife and I rebuilt our legacy by opening several franchise restaurants. We have been able to help our sons through college and give back to the Refuge and other nonprofits.

These sacrifices were not mine alone. Starting the Refuge upended my whole family. Each one of my family members has sacrificed as well. My wife had to leave her whole life behind so that I could pursue the vision. We pulled our kids out of private school. My oldest child was in seventh grade at the time, and while he attended a great Christian school that he loved, he had to say good-bye to all his friends when we moved.

We gave up our livelihood and our nice suburban home in order to relocate to a poor Appalachian town where we knew no one. This was a huge culture shock. Our children's new classmates had grown up in poverty the likes of which our kids had never seen. Some of the children walked around town barefoot because they had no shoes.

This poverty was not confined to our neighbors. *We* were now poor. I gave up a high salary for a life in which we struggled to put food on the table. This was not pretend. We were right in the thick of it with all our savings poured into the Refuge.

My family wasn't exactly happy about these changes, but I had cast my vision to them first. They understood what we were doing and why. They were all on board and ready to make the sacrifice too. My wife and I raised our kids with the Christian values of service and charity. They got a crash course in loving thy neighbor! But it wasn't easy on them.

Our children continued to sacrifice as they grew older. They served at the Refuge as kids and still do so as adults. They have given up jobs and other opportunities to keep serving here.

My son is a musician. He started playing guitar and singing at the age of thirteen and has played in worship bands for many years. He is also the founder and pastor of a church in Columbus that provides a community for our men once they leave the Refuge. This is how he now serves. His sacrifice has been every bit as big as mine. He placed his musical aspirations on hold in order to put the men of the Refuge first, abandoning a serious music career.

A few years ago, he was offered a full-time music position to play for a major church in Seattle. He would have been able to record music, play music full time, and even go on tour. This was an opportunity for him to realize a lifelong dream.

He turned down the offer.

His dream may have been to play worship music, but his *calling* was to work with the men of the Refuge through a community inner-city church. For that, he was willing to sacrifice. He had developed relationships in the ministry that he could not leave. He had responsibilities he could not abandon. He felt unable to leave his post at the church. This was his sacrifice. He gave up a career in music to stay in a rough area of the city and serve our men. This was his and his wife's choice, their sacrifice. I never pushed them. They felt that this was their calling as much as it was mine.

Many people involved with the Refuge have made similar sacrifices. They came on and found their calling within our ministry. They made sacrifices just like I did. There is not a man or woman who works with the Refuge who hasn't made a sacrifice to serve here. We have had men leave the ministry and return to serve. Often they return having pursued advanced degrees in the interim. They give up careers and jobs. More than one director has brought his wife along when he moved here to serve the men.

We make these sacrifices because our callings are bigger than ourselves. Our callings are more important than our own lives. This is why we sacrifice. Our personal happiness, while not unimportant, is beside the point. Your calling is not even about you; it is greater than yourself. This is why it is so rewarding to sacrifice and give.

"Stuff" Is Just Stuff

While following your calling is quite possibly the most rewarding thing you will ever do, sacrifice can still be difficult, painful, and scary. Giving up everything you have and know to step out into the unknown is daunting.

I have three pieces of advice to offer.

The first is not to worry about giving up material possessions and base comforts. Many people focus on material sacrifices. This is understandable. People tend to link material possessions with success and security. You don't need as much money or as many conveniences as you think you do to be secure and happy. Although God has blessed us as we have had seasons of abasement and abundance, we have had to learn to be content in either. God blesses us all, and having materials isn't wrong as long as the materials don't own our hearts.

I don't mean to minimize the sacrifice. Giving up all your stuff and your salary *is* hard. Accepting a lower standard of living is a shock. However, these things are ultimately not all that valuable or important. Big houses, fancy clothes, nice cars, and all the other trappings of wealth are simply not as important as following your passion and heeding God's call. They won't ultimately make you happy anyway. Material possessions provide a cheap satisfaction that will pale in comparison to the satisfaction and sense of purpose you will derive from pursuing your true calling and passion.

This allows for a change of perspective. Instead of focusing on what you are giving up, focus on what you will gain. Heeding your calling is enormously fulfilling. No job has ever given me the sense of pride and satisfaction that I get from working at the Refuge. Every morning, I wake up and go to a place that God built, and I witness the positive impact we are having on people's lives and the community. Seeing the change we help the men make in their lives is indescribable. It is such a beautiful thing! God may also do for you as He has done for us, and bless you along the way through other means. What an awesome God we serve.

I understand that a good salary buys more than just "stuff." It provides financial security. Money buys insurance against misfortune and can make us feel safe, especially when we have a family to care for.

However, safety is just an illusion. There are no guarantees in life; you can lose it all in an instant. You can lose your job. You can have a crippling accident. A sudden illness can bankrupt you. A natural catastrophe can wipe out your home. Markets collapse. Whole industries go bust. There is no *truly* safe path in life, not really.

So why not take a risk and follow your dreams? Why not heed a passion and calling? Not following your passion puts you at a 100 percent risk of leading the wrong life and failing to honor God. Your life will be better anyway when you stop living for stuff and start living to serve.

Trust That God Will Provide

My second piece of advice is to have faith in God. He *will* provide. When the road grows dark, he will show you the way. As was discussed in the previous chapter, you will have doubts and fears. You must push through these and carry forward. Do not let the fear of the unknown derail you. Do not let the fear of sacrifice keep you from heeding your call. If you believe in God, and that He is giving you a calling, you cannot go wrong in heeding that call.

This advice also applies to fears about sacrifices that must be made. Trust in God to see you through and take care of you. You will find a practical way to make things work. Yes, you may have to make some sacrifices in order to follow your calling, but things will work out in the end. God will provide for you. He may not provide us with a high salary and financial independence, but we must have faith that we will have all we need.

I am not saying that you must condemn yourself to a lifetime of poverty. Sacrifice is not about making a show of frugalness. You simply need to be willing to make the sacrifices necessary to pursue your calling. That may mean putting your career on hold. It may mean that you take a pay cut. It doesn't have to mean that you will be living on rice and beans forever.

Have faith in God and the future, and you may end up with *more* than you need. That is what happened to my family. We are now better off financially than we ever were before coming to Vinton County. While I certainly don't profit from the Refuge, we have done well financially by opening restaurant franchises. We noted that the county didn't have a single fast-food restaurant, so we opened a sandwich shop to make money while building the Refuge. My wife ran the shop while I worked with the men. She now manages twelve sandwich shops, and we are again financially secure.

This is something we never would have considered before coming to Vinton County. My wife didn't know anything about restaurants. However, we had to put food on the table and send our kids to college, so we looked around for opportunities. The county is sparsely populated and underdeveloped economically. The whole county has only one stoplight. Businesses are few and far between, but we saw an opportunity and ran with it.

Have faith that the Lord will often provide for you, and have faith that you can provide for yourself. Life is full of unexpected turns, and new opportunities will present themselves. I walked away from a successful business to start the Refuge. We thought we were going to be poor, but, on the contrary, we now have more than we ever did before.

We are able to funnel much of the surplus back into the Refuge. We are now not only the Refuge's founders; we are also one of the ministry's biggest donors. This is a beautiful cycle! We serve the community, the community gives back, and we are then able to give even more back to the community.

We didn't plan for any of this; we couldn't have. Making money was never the point. We just trusted that God would provide. We committed ourselves to the calling, made the necessary sacrifices, took opportunities on the side as they appeared, and had faith. God did the rest.

Figuring out how to provide for yourself while you pursue your calling is no different from any other aspect of pursuing the vision. You don't have to know your next move to get started. Don't jump into things blindly, of course. Plan carefully and make the proper preparations, but understand that things will change as you go. You will have to adjust your course and figure out some things as you go. Have faith that God will show you the way.

The High Price of Inaction

My third piece of advice is to consider the price of not acting. It is easy to focus on what we must give up when we throw ourselves headlong into a life of service. However, take a moment to really think about the price of *not* taking action.

We often have to sacrifice to heed a calling, but the price of not heeding the call may be steeper still. Deciding to play it safe and stick with the status quo may feel easier in the moment. You don't have to give up anything now. Your comfortable life can carry on as it has been.

But imagine yourself decades from now having given up your calling before you even got started. Imagine being old, on your deathbed, and you haven't pursued your passion. You haven't pursued God's calling. Close your eyes and picture yourself looking back at your life. Imagine having never done this thing that is burning in your heart. Now imagine no longer having the time in life to do so.

How do you feel?

Would you be OK with this? Or, do you already feel the pang of future regret?

This is ultimately what sealed the deal for me. I thought about looking back on my life without ever having given this a shot. I couldn't bear the thought. I couldn't accept the notion of my having ignored God's call.

Yes, I was scared to fail. I was afraid I was making a mistake. I understood the huge sacrifices that I would have to make—all I'd have to forfeit on behalf of my family. I was afraid I would do all of that and still fail.

But ultimately, I knew that failing was better than not trying and never knowing. It was better to make a mistake and seem a fool than to risk not heeding what felt like God's call. I would someday have to answer for my actions. I would rather have to explain making a mistake and wasting my time than risk ignoring God's plan for me.

I don't want to contend with "what ifs" at the end of my life. I want to be able to look back and know with certainty that, while I didn't play the game perfectly, I at least showed up for the right game. I want to know that I went for it. I want to know that I didn't shy away from my passions, and that I wasn't too scared to serve.

Above all, I had to take this path because I needed to confirm that my faith was real. I needed to see if service and God and spirituality were really things for which I stood. If I wasn't willing to make sacrifices, then everything I represented was a charade. I would be a Christian in name only. Taking action was necessary to test my faith. If service wasn't important to me, then what was I doing wasting time in church? If

I couldn't make a sacrifice for God, then how important was He to me, really?

Ultimately, I had to put my trust in God in order to know if all of this was real. My vision was a chance to put my faith to the test. I wasn't content to "play" church. I wanted to test my limits, my faith, and my devotion. I needed to see if God really was acting in my life.

I went for it, and I was not disappointed. I can now report back with certainty that God is acting in my life. Divine confirmation and spiritual markers are my proof. How I feel is my proof. The life I have created is my proof. The spiritual community I created and threw myself into is all the proof I need.

CONCLUSION

A Call to Service

I hope this book has been meaningful to you in some way, and that there is something here that resonates deeply with you. Perhaps it will even inspire you to act.

That is the only purpose of this book. I want to inspire people to act, get involved, and help serve their fellow man to the glory of God. I have no hard sell. I am not trying to "franchise" the Refuge, and I'm not trying to recruit you into our ministry.

The Refuge is not a business, and it is not something from which I profit. It is not about making money; it is about honoring God and serving man. It is about heeding a calling, spreading the Gospel, and helping others walk with God. In that respect, this book is no different from the work I do at the Refuge. I want to help you walk with God and live a life of service according to the Scripture.

On that note, I want to leave you with a challenge: **Look deep into yourself and ask yourself what God put you here on Earth to do.** God has a purpose for you. He wants you to honor and serve. He has a calling for you.

That calling is no mystery. Your calling isn't a puzzle that needs to be solved. You simply need to speak with God. Look inside yourself, examine your life, look for spiritual confirmations and markers, and see where God is pulling you. Talk to Him, ask Him for His guidance, and be ready to listen.

Once you know your calling, heed the call. And do it today. Don't wait until next year, or even until tomorrow. Get started right now—even if that just means telling somebody about what you want to do or writing it down on paper.

I want to personally offer you my help and counsel while you get started. I am more than happy to talk to anyone about anything in this book. I am always looking for new ways to honor God and serve others. The way I *most* love to serve others is by helping them serve others too. This creates a snowball effect that lets us build up the glory of God's kingdom together.

Maybe you want to start a place like the Refuge. Let's talk about that. I have a lot of advice to give in addition to that which appears in this book. Maybe you want to start some different kind of ministry or organization, and I'll probably have advice to give you about that too. Maybe you have some other way of serving, perhaps at the Refuge or perhaps in your own way. I am happy to talk about whatever idea you may have in mind.

My ultimate motive in writing this book was to inspire others to start Refuge-like ministries throughout the world. I believe Jesus Christ and biblical truth is the solution to the addiction issue. We need more opportunities like the Refuge and we should be involved to be aware of the needs of our culture. May all that I have shared glorify my Father and exalt the name of Jesus, not myself, the Refuge, or anything else. May God be the Glory!!!

Whatever your cause, whatever your goals or methods, whatever you need to ask—feel free to reach out and find me. I can be contacted via email at tthompson@therefugeohio.org.

Thank you for reading, and God bless.

A journey with God

Many prayer walks and times of intimacy with God

Sleeping and eating quarters

The transformation center

*Our place of baptisms and the encounter
with the butterflies*

108 acres of "holy ground"

A time of Prayer during our 1st encounter

*This is the Thompson family when
they started the ministry*

This is the Columbus property

This is the Lancaster property

*A remenant of the 2500 men
that have entered the Refuge*

Thankful for our food and all of Gods provision

7 CORE VALUES of the REFUGE

These core values create the culture of The Refuge. Are the men ready for The Refuge?

1 Commitment to God

Matthew 22.37 "Jesus replied, 'You must love the Lord your God with all your heart, all your soul, and all your mind.'"

☐ I give everything and myself as I commit to 100% in my calling and my motive is to please my Heavenly Father.

☐ I am truly responsible for my actions and outcomes and own everything that takes place in my life.

☐ I am accountable for my results and I know that for things to change, first I must transform and become Jesus Christ-like.

☐ I am committed to the journey of discipleship!

2 Relational with Others

Matthew 22.39 "A second is equally important: 'Love your neighbor as yourself.'"

☐ I am committed to the Vision, Mission, Culture and success of Refuge Ministries, its Elders, the Staff and its Men at all times.

☐ I am a team player and team leader. I do, to the best of my abilities, whatever it takes to stay together and achieve team goals.

☐ I focus on co-operation and always come to a resolution, not a compromise.

☐ I am flexible in my work and able to change if what I'm doing is not working.

☐ I ask for help when I need it and I am compassionate to others who ask me.

☐ I speak positively of my fellow Elders, the Staff and the Men at Refuge Ministries in both public and private.

☐ I speak with good purpose using empowering and positive conversation. I never use or listen to slander or gossip.

☐ I acknowledge what is being said as true for the speaker at that moment and I take responsibility for responses to my communication.

☐ I always apologize for any upsets first and then look for a solution. I only discuss concerns in private with the person involved.

☐ I view my life as a journey to be enjoyed and appreciated and I create an atmosphere of fun and happiness so all around me enjoy it as well.

Teachable / Patience

3

2 Timothy 2.2 **"You have heard me teach things that have been confirmed by many reliable witnesses. Now teach these truths to other trustworthy people who will be able to pass them on to others."**

Good enough, isn't good enough!

☐ I always deliver on my responsibilities with exceptional quality that add value to all involved for the long term.

☐ I look for ways to do more with less and stay on a path of constant and never ending improvement and innovation.

☐ I learn from my mistakes. I consistently learn, grow and master so that I can help my fellow Elders, Staff and men learn, grow and master too.

☐ I impart practical and useable knowledge rather than just theory.

Honest / Authentic

James 5.16 "Confess your sins to each other and pray for each other so that you may be healed. The earnest prayer of a righteous person has great power and produces wonderful results."

☐ I always speak the truth. What I promise is what I deliver.

☐ I only make agreements (verbal and written), with myself and others that I am willing and intend to keep.

☐ I communicate potential broken agreements at the first opportunity and I clear up all broken agreements immediately.

☐ I am consistent in my actions so my fellow Elders can feel comfortable in dealing with me at all times.

Gratitude / Thankful

Philippines 4.6 Don't worry about anything; instead, pray about everything. Tell God what you need, and thank him for all he has done.

☐ I am a truly grateful person.

☐ I am so grateful to have God in my life. I thank others and show appreciation often and in many ways, so those around me know how much I appreciate everything and everyone I have in my life.

☐ I celebrate my blessings and the blessings of the team.

☐ I consistently catch myself and other people doing things right and affirm them.

Courage / Faith

Hebrews 11.6 And it is impossible to please God without faith. Anyone who wants to come to him must believe that God exists and that he rewards those who sincerely seek him.

☐ I am a blessed person, I desire God's blessing and I am easily able to both give and receive it.

☐ I allow blessing in all areas of my life by expecting from my Heavenly Father, respecting my own self worth and that of all others.

☐ I am rewarded to the level that I create abundance for others and I accept that abundance only shows up in my life to the level at which I show up and am faithful.

Work Ethic / Faithfulness / Stewardship

1 Thessalonians 4.11-12 "Make it your goal to live a quiet life, minding your own business and working with your hands, just as we instructed you before. Then people who are not Christians will respect the way you live, and you will not need to depend on others."

☐ I totally focus my thoughts, energy and attention on the successful outcome of whatever I am doing with the skills, talents and gifts God has given me.

☐ I am willing to win and allow others to win.

☐ At all times, I display my inner pride, prosperity, competence and personal assurance in Jesus Christ.

☐ I am a successful ambassador of Jesus Christ.

☐ I will take responsibility to utilize stewardship practices and stay within the budget and work in unity with the team to become a sustainable ministry model.

☐ I will not over spend and I will look for innovative ways to cut costs and generate revenue.

☐ I will support the checks, balances and measurements for financial accountability to display a responsible steward to the men and the Lord.

☐ I will hold myself and others accountable to treat all assets with the utmost respect due to the understanding the Lord owns all that we have.

CPSIA information can be obtained
at www.ICGtesting.com
Printed in the USA
FSHW021458130421
80302FS